KNEWGOAT

A Black Man's Journey To Greatness In The Hell That Is America

MARQUISE THOMPSON

Marquise Thompson, Author
Knewgoat: A Black Man's Journey to Greatness in the Hell
that is America Previous title: My Refusal
Available for purchase at www.knewgoat.com or
www.Amazon.com

Edited by Auketria Manor On Writer's Block
www.onwritersblock.net
Cover Design by Michael Corvin IG: @bookcoverdesign_

Connect with Marquise Thompson on Instagram, Facebook
and Twitter: @Knewgoat

This work is dedicated to the memory of my friend Chavin Kendrick. I kept my word. You told me to write a sequel to My Refusal. Mission accomplished. Fly high, King.

Contents

1

LIFE IS THE GENESIS OF DEATH

Where do our souls reside and soar from before making their grand entrance into the womb? Are our souls sheltered and asleep in an unknown dark cocoon before we are conceived? Where do our souls drift away to when fate taps the wristwatch of death to indicate our time on Earth has expired? Perhaps we return to our essence, a oneness with the goodness of God and the universe that we seem to lose sight of once we are born. Maybe the unknown becomes known.

Rich or poor, intelligent or dumb, lighter or darker hue, it all matters naught when the angel of death whispers, "come with me" to your soul. When the grim reaper decides to draw the curtains of life nigh, we all have the same say so – no say so. The silent darkness that encompasses death illuminates the joy and beauty of life that every living individual must leave behind someday.

We are taught to appreciate and cherish each second as

if it's our last since being born is presumed to be the beginning of an amazing blessing called life that we are only fortunate enough to experience once. All the special moments shared with loving parents, grandparents and friends we love like family reduces our finite time on Earth. The good times that we take for granted, including the beams of warmth bestowed upon our God-given melanin by the sun, bring us closer to our final breath. Closer to our final destination of no longer existing in the physical form in the not-so-distant future. How can life be this incredible blessing and amalgamation of unique experiences only lived once, but also the Genesis of Death? Perhaps our souls on ice are akin to water, liquid in the womb that becomes ice when we are born and then vapor that drifts into the wandering tides of blowing wind when we pass away.

During my adolescent years, I once asked my pops, "Do you believe in heaven or hell?" With no hesitation, my dad swiftly replied, "Son, I don't know about heaven, but I certainly believe in hell. Forget believing in it Hassan, I know for a fact that hell exists." My father's surprising proclamation generated tremors of shock that shook me to my core. His sentiment caught me off guard because his perspective directly conflicted with the teachings that my mother taught my younger brother and me during our formative years. During my childhood, my mom made it abundantly clear that she believed good people went to heaven when they die and bad people joined God's nemesis, the father of all lies, Satan, in hell when their lives expired. Perhaps my mother had forgotten to share her wisdom and knowledge of the afterlife with my father, who believed something completely different about life and death. As I reminisced about my mom's teachings of the afterlife, my dad's brown eyes and black pupils intently peered in my direction as I pedantically contemplated his frightening words. I could tell he was waiting to see if his shocking statement would elicit a well thought out response or an emotional nonsensical volcanic eruption from me. As I slowly came to grips with my dad's perspective, cumulus clouds began to brainstorm raindrops of dissent. After a few moments of silence, I finally mustered up the courage to question the older version of myself, the man that raised me—the man that I idolized more than anyone else, the person whose words I typically accepted as gospel without question.

"Pops, if hell is a place that you have never been to, how can you be so sure it's real?" I cautiously inquired as I attempted to whisk him and our frightening conversation into a corner of quandary and deep contemplation that would end our exchange. "Son, America being hell for a black man, is simpler than you think. I've resided in hell for forty-plus years. And you have resided in Satan's abode for at least eighteen something years. Life for a black man in America is the epitome of hell," he calmly stated while harshly pressing his right index finger into my chest. I could tell my father was torn between continuing his soliloquy or shifting to a more lighthearted topic, something that I was better versed in, like sports, perhaps. After a few moments of silence elapsed, my father decided not to take our conversation in a different direction and expanded upon his initial position.

"Hassan, you're public enemy number 1 to everyone here and don't you ever forget that. Society blames you for all the problems here. If being a black man in America isn't hell, I don't know what is," he stated as a matter of fact.

"America, for you is hell, and as a black man, you have been deemed the serpent of sin that will never walk upright again. Even if heaven is real, as a black man in America, you have more in common with being surrounded by fire, brimstone and devils than you do with levitating with Angels in the clouds above streets made of gold."

As I pondered my father's assessment of life being hell for a black man in America, he decided to share more of his unique perspective.

"Think about it. Who's always blamed and painted as the perpetrator of senseless violence?" My dad held out the palm of his hand and flipped it from the white side to highlight his bronze complexion. While pointing at his brown skin, my father stated, "As it pertains to violence, any and everybody that looks just like you, me and your younger brother Deuce will always fit the description. Why is that?" he asked before pausing to allow me to digest his words. "Our acts of violence and resistance are consistently highlighted and denigrated, while the violent acts of hate from others are continuously justified or outright ignored. Cops can kill a black person at any time for just existing and the injustice system of America will say he or she did something to deserve it. Think about it. What do Emmett Till, Ahmaud Arbery and Breonna Taylor have in common? They were unjustly killed, and then their character was assassinated before their bodies even made it to the graveyard. We have seen state violence sanctioned and justified against us for centuries. Yet, you and I, the offspring of those oppressed for four hundred years, the survivors of the transatlantic slave trade atrocities, the forgiving marchers that walked in peace with the likes of Dr. King, remain the sole face of violence.

"The past and present hate that society directs at our people has existed since America's inception," he continued. "In the summer of 1926, two young boys who were siblings, the Carter brothers, were lynched for no reason at all. They never had the chance to see their dreams materialize. They never had an opportunity to migrate from youth to adulthood—the chance to migrate from the treacherous South to experience *The Warmth of Other Suns* described by Isabel

Wilkerson. On top of that, the hate from this country isn't just directed at our sons; it's so vitriolic that it has claimed the lives of countless black girls as well."

My dad took a few deep breaths before listing the young girls' names that were murdered during the 16th Street Baptist Church bombing as tears began to wail in his eyes. It was as if the smoke and fire from the white supremacists' bomb had formed the names Addie Mae Collins, Cynthia Wesley, Carole Robertson and Carol McNair in red blood right before my father's eyes. He slowly traced letters in the air as he painfully muttered the names of each little black girl who lost their lives in the 16th Street Baptist Church bombing.

"When the veil of the Ku Klux Klan was finally lifted, it shocked many to see that it was the everyday American using the white hood to mask their hate. People that previously hid their faces underneath the sheets remained or assimilated into positions of power in the judicial and policing systems that allowed them to legally torture us without wearing hoods."

My dad typically kept his emotions in check, but he struggled to maintain his composure whenever our people's plight was discussed. After regaining his composure somewhat, he continued:

"You ever ask yourself why a mugshot is always included on the nightly news when someone black is accused of a crime?" I could tell my dad wanted to venture further down the rabbit hole of how the news media specializes in and purposely markets the black man as the face of crime and someone who should be feared by all. But, instead of venturing down the rabbit hole of the mugshot marketing tactics utilized by media outlets, my dad shifted his analysis to debunking the ever so present myth of black on black violence.

"Hassan, the violence that exists in Tree Port and some of our communities is genuinely the byproduct of depriving young kings of an opportunity to discover their real crowns. A fair chance for young boys to grow and learn from their mistakes without being criminalized the very first moment they emerge from their mother's wombs. Instead of being welcomed to a world full of light and love, our kids enter an even darker environment than their first home, a world that's even dimmer than the womb. Sadly, the darkness that our kids are born into never goes away; it just becomes more pervasive and difficult to deal with as we age. The darkness that I'm speaking of remains firmly intact until a cop car pulls us over and shines the bright light of America's predilection for injustice upon us for driving while black. We are disproportionately pulled over, searched and arrested to confirm the narrative that we are natural-born criminals. We are targeted to uphold the belief that black on black crime is real and substantiated.

"Black on black crime is a myth that is leveraged to distract and guilt us into believing that we deserve to be mistreated by police, judges and the entire judicial system. Across all ethnicities, crime and violence within a specific community are based on proximity, nothing more and nothing less. There's a symbiotic relationship between despair and violence that society hates to acknowledge. It's easy to castigate and reduce us to being defective serpents that don't have the wherewithal to value or appreciate life. According to them, it's in our nature to kill one another. And don't even get me started on this movement and narrative that black men don't love black women. Eighty-nine percent of us who do choose to marry select a black queen as our helpmate. But somehow, someway, there's this persistent and pervasive myth that we don't love our women. Is there room to improve how black men treat and protect our women? Absolutely! But do not tell me that we don't love our women when the facts say otherwise. We love and appreciate our black Queens, and we must make sure our words, and most importantly, our actions consistently affirm that love."

As Billy Paul's classic *Let the Dollars Circulate* blared from my father's navy-blue Acura, he took a few brief moments to catch his breath and further gather his remaining thoughts.

As Billy Paul crooned about letting the dollars circulate and the unethical actions of politicians, my father continued,

"Do you know who America blamed for the recession in the 80s? The black man. "Those crazy motha……," he said before pausing as his voice blended into the buzzing whisking wind as if it was a classic DJ Premier sample scratch. Somehow my dad managed to stop his tongue when he realized he would be swearing in front of his young son. My dad inhaled deeply and took a deep breath before continuing with his train of thought that had been briefly derailed. "They say the recession happened because we didn't sell enough of that Iran Contra garbage that the government funneled to our community. Can you believe that the black man caused the recession of the 1980s because he didn't sell enough crack to his own people? *Bleep* Ronald Reagan and may his soul feel what it's like to be a black man in America—may his soul feel hell."

As my dad's voice echoed down the halls of memory lane, I began to contemplate the complexity of the man who raised me. My father was astute and charming to most, yet he never seemed capable of truly clasping the joy of life that seemed to be within his arm's reach. His marriage to my mom was occasionally good but never great. On Fridays, when times were good, he would two-step while sipping red wine and twirl my mom around as classics from Marvin Gaye and Tammi Terrell blared from his record player. I would look on and nod my head to the tunes as he'd spin my mom around and send her for a dip with one hand while miraculously balancing his wine with his other hand without spilling a drop. I missed those times dearly and would frequently imagine dancing like my dad and mom with my forever lady one day.

While my dad and mom's relationship had its share of ups and downs, his relationships with me and my younger brother consistently remained in good standing. Deuce and I admired our father a great deal. It was seldom, if ever that he let us down. But alas, from my father's perspective, he wanted our relationship to be a bit more real than it was. Out of courtesy and respect for my mom, he seemed to refrain from sharing his unfiltered thoughts with us at times. Our relationship was real but not authentic enough in his estimation. His knowledge of the world and its obstacles was extremely refined and rooted in realism. Yet, he consistently made moves that set him and our family back. It's like his skepticism of the world deflated his big dreams and hopes for a better life into a nightmare that he was unable to escape or awaken from. The more knowledgeable he became, the more defiant and convinced he became that his sins were not shortcomings but merely uncontrollable and inconsequential results that transpired from living life.

While my father had his myriad of faults that he never fully conquered, he still managed to teach me a great deal about life. He taught me the truth about us. He taught me the history that the world conspired to erase. He taught me the nuance of understanding Tree Port's street politics. My father taught me how to remain true to myself at all times and how to confront and manage peer pressure in an effective manner. "Hassan, always be true to yourself. No one knows the real you better than you. Son, the trek that you are on, the journey to greatness, it all starts within. All within," he would say as he pointed at my heart. I can't recall many instances of my life where he explicitly taught me right from wrong, but he still managed to share gems that helped me become a better person. Instead of teaching me the difference between right and wrong, he often shared his abstract philosophies and spoke in parables that seemingly left me figuring out how to navigate life on my own accord. My dad was biblical, in some ways. He embraced his calling of being a complicated philosophical thinker and griot who frequently constructed quotes filled with gems that most misunderstood. One of his favorite sayings was the Sun (not son) of God technically owned everything but died broke on Earth. Even the traitor Judas Iscariot died with more material possessions than Jesus—30 pieces of silver for the coward who betrayed the one known as *Savior.*

One of the few things that I recall my father explicitly telling me pertained to my survival. He once made it crystal clear how I should manage the ownership of my pistol. With no ambiguity or room for misinterpretation, my father stated that I should never draw a weapon unless I planned to etch death on a bullet and permanently remove a name from the book of life. "Don't ever pull the strap on a person unless you plan on doing work right then and there. If you draw down on a sucker, be sure to send him to his maker right then and there. No further discussions or negotiations are permitted once you raise your gun towards another man. If I ever pull my gun on you, Hassan, run immediately because that means that I deemed it necessary to murder my son like Abraham was commanded to do to Isaac before the ram emerged from the bush. You can rest assured that any man you let walk away after brandishing a weapon will view you as a lifelong nemesis. And the next time that person sees you, fear will drive them to plant a bullet in your brain. Kiss your life goodbye if you ever pull a weapon and decide not to use it. God forbid you ever pull a pistol on someone and decide not to use it," he stated as he shook his head profusely. After hearing my father's advice on guns, I glanced at the twenty-two married to his waist and wondered how many souls it had divorced from life. I suppose my dad sharing his wisdom on how to kill would have made him a contender for father of the year to most in Tree Port, as making it to the age of the lost years of Jesus' life that were omitted from the Bible was considered miraculous.

2

SERPENT OF SIN

I had always heard that before you perish, your life flashes before your eyes. I had managed to make it to adulthood by narrowly escaping the hook of the grim reaper's sickle a time or two before. Still, it seemed the time had finally come for me to discover the real truth regarding life flashing before our eyes before we die. As I contemplated my father's words of wisdom regarding guns, my best friend and I circled one another with our pistols pointed directly at each other. How do friends who are like brothers reach a point of contentiousness such as this? I suppose our experiences in life and perspective on how to resolve problems best brought us to this point. If there was one thing that being raised in Tree Port taught me, it was that some issues could only be resolved with a bullet. That was finally the case for two Tree Port legends. We had reached an unfortunate impasse that would only allow one of us to emerge as the victor.

This showdown was the point of no return. There wasn't enough air on Earth for us both to continue breathing.

As nervous adrenaline caused my left hand to shake and wobble, I tightly clutched my nine while my father's words about only pulling a gun to send someone to their maker continuously echoed in my head. For some odd reason, I was more fearful of pulling the trigger to murder my best friend than I was of staring down the barrel of death that he had dangerously positioned inches from snatching my life away. I had suffered a tremendous loss before, which could have been prevented if I had reacted differently. I didn't want to make that same mistake again. Taking the life of someone who deserves to live is no small burden to bear.

As my best friend and I continued to circle one another, it was as if everything was happening at one hundred miles per hour while simultaneously moving slower than a crippled elderly snail operating on CP time. Suddenly, I saw my best friend's finger move half an inch and squeeze the trigger. His gun jolted upward as a murderous bullet emerged from the chamber and started traveling towards the front of my cranium. A millisecond before the bullet penetrated the first centimeter of my skin, I smelled the gun smoke for a brief moment. As the bullet raced towards me, I had a chance to do what we are taught to do when we presume that we are dying. Ask God for the forgiveness of my sins and accept Jesus as my Lord and Savior. What type of person passes on the opportunity to pray for eternal salvation before their death?

Just in case heaven and hell exist, it makes sense to quickly repent before a treacherous bullet ends your life, right? Could I truly be this stupid? Just say, "Lord, I believe your son died for my sins, please permit me into heaven and grant me eternal life," or something to that effect. Since I was choosing to waste my final seconds being analytical, instead of asking God for forgiveness for my sins, I might as well have been JFK riding with the top off in Dallas right before his assassination. JFK had no idea a bullet was enroute to terminate his life; therefore, he was never allowed to plead for his soul via prayer and final repentance. Life was granting me my last opportunity to do just that. For no rhyme or reason, I declined to pray for eternal salvation in my final moments. I figured if I hadn't earned my way into heaven by way of my life's merits and how I treated others; why attempt to cheat my way into the pearly gates in my final moments?

B-O-O-M was the last earthly sound I heard before my soul emerged from my bloody body and began to transition to what I assumed to be heaven or hell. The process of dying is rapid yet slow, smooth yet bumpy, peaceful yet unnerving. Leaving Earth is hard to describe. It's akin to riding first class on an Emirates international flight while simultaneously flying economy on Spirit Airlines on a domestic flight. It's a transition that no living being can articulate as you have to die first to experience it, and as we all know, death offers our souls no roundtrip tickets back to Earth. The lone person who could have explained death was probably Lazarus as the Son of God once resurrected him after all.

As I struggled to determine if I was headed north to heaven or south to hell, the highs and lows of my life began to scroll by like a brilliant Marvel Universe cinematic recap crafted by Stan Lee. The highs were rather impressive and exhilarating. Emerging from the dreadful blood-drenched streets of Tree Port to become a productive citizen who achieved financial security felt as unfathomable in death as it did in life. Reliving the lows was appalling. Seeing those who mattered the most to me die a second time and fully accepting the fact I had fallen victim to the same violence that had claimed the lives of so many brothers and sisters before me was heart-wrenching and painful. For all that I accomplished professionally, I was unable to avoid becoming just another brother who greeted the graveyard before his mother and father.

As the highlight reel of my tenure on Earth neared its conclusion, my belief that I was transitioning north and not south began to blossom. I felt no fire and didn't smell hellish volcanic remnants. Maybe it was a sign that I was headed to the pearly gates of heaven. I don't know if you can technically pray once you are deceased, but my most recent prayer appeared to be answered as my soul's flight came to an abrupt conclusion. So, this was heaven, beings that I recognized were draped in attire that I can't describe and seemed to be having the times of their lives. The best of the best were tending to instruments they had mastered during their lifetimes. I saw Elijah McClain strumming his violin as the keys of a silver piano moved up and down and played Beethoven's Moonlight Sonata classic. Individuals who appeared to be Fannie Lou Hamer, Miles Davis, Duke Ellington and Bob Marley were having an in-depth conversation about music from what I could discern of their voices. I couldn't make out much of their interaction, but I did hear Mr. Marley say, "Exodus," to Duke Ellington. Perhaps Duke had asked Bob Marley what his greatest record was.

As I continued to walk, I spotted a young boy I remembered, an innocent child who lost his life at a young age due to the senseless violence in Tree Port.

As my soul struggled to grasp any and everything about heaven, a Being that looked like an ageless version of myself started speaking. "It's time," the Being stated.

To fully understand my death, you must first understand what led to my death. Life led to my death. Had I never been born, I would have never died. Had I never died, I would have never been born. Life is the Genesis of Death.

Life is funny. I spent my whole life trying to become the best version of myself. I devoted a substantial amount of my time and energy to scaling mountains of doubt in my quest to reach heights that seemed unreachable. I suppose my goal was to accomplish what many deemed impossible, all in the name of making my parents and younger brother beam with pride and joy and to perhaps leave wealth behind for future generations of my lineage. My quest for success made sense when I was living but didn't materialize to anything of substance once I passed away. What I thought meant so much while living didn't seem to matter once I was deceased.

Death has a way of shining light into the crevices of places that we prefer to remain dark. Life is riddled with non-stop lessons and clichés that we believe have the capacity to change our minds and ultimately transform our lives if we follow the breadcrumbs outlined by "successful" people closely enough. From the moment we are born, we're taught that what we accomplish today impacts our future. If you make the right strategic moves and sacrifices today, you can live like a king or queen in the future, they say. Sound advice for the living that makes a ton of sense until you perish. What's the point of making sacrifices today if your tomorrow won't even matter? I suppose the point is to build and leave a legacy behind that lives on when we are no longer present on Earth in the physical form. Maybe our purpose is to leave a legacy that shines as a beacon of hope to those from similar circumstances as they aspire to achieve what feels unfathomable. In our absence, perhaps we can still impact those left behind positively.

Have you ever pondered your real motivation for being the person you are? Would you still treat people right if there was no promised reward of heaven to believe in? Are the good works and charitable actions we perform while living solely motivated by the fear of eternal condemnation? If we were never taught about the existence of heaven and hell, would we still try to be the best versions of ourselves?

As I reminisced and evaluated the motivating factors that shaped how I lived my life, a life that was shorter than an unlucky leprechaun, I transitioned back to analyzing what the ageless version of myself meant when he originally stated, "It's time." And that's when the Eternal Being continued speaking.

"It is now that the wages of your sins and shortcomings are to be weighed. The true intent behind your daily actions, negative and good deeds are about to be judged and assessed. Walk with me," the Being stated.

As we began to move, I inquired, "Where are we going?" The ageless Being peered in my direction and stared beyond my heart and soul and stated, "Nowhere, but everywhere."

It was at that moment that I started to contemplate the true meaning of life again. At conception, are we projected to Earth for a great cause or mission that we don't understand? Do we ignore our real purpose because we become too enamored with the evil and greed of this dog-eat-dog world? Is life merely a journey that presents us with opportunities and learning experiences that challenges us to become the best versions of ourselves? What if life is an opportunity for us to sprinkle our souls with seeds of greatness that evolve into compassion, love and humanity's overall betterment? Do we circumvent our destiny by refusing to make the appropriate sacrifices that will nourish our development and growth? Or is life just a constant conflict with depression, pain and hurt that we as humans use as an excuse to inflict harm on one another? Perhaps life is just the prelude to death and nothingness that our self-aggrandizement and arrogance refuse to allow us to accept peacefully? Is it our human arrogance that has convinced us that we are so important that life on Earth can't be the end for us?

So many things that we assume mean everything means absolutely nothing. So many moments that we take for granted mean everything.

As I followed the ageless Being, I couldn't tell if I was walking, flying, or perhaps even gliding. I had no wings, at least none that I could discern or see. Yet, I felt like a soaring eagle navigating the endless sky with ease, weaving between and above clouds. As we marched or flew towards our unknown destination, I started asking questions that I always wanted to know the answer to.

"Does every person who asks for forgiveness of their sins and acknowledge Yahweh as their Lord and Savior make it to heaven no matter what? For example, Trump sentenced an absurd amount of people to death with his idiotic response to a global pandemic. He's culpable for the deaths of hundreds of thousands of people. You mean to tell me if he decides to ask for forgiveness before his death, his racism and countless acts of ignorance will be forgiven, and Trump will be granted entrance to heaven? How can a last-minute request for forgiveness hold more weight than living a good life? How is that fair?" I asked the enlightened Eternal Version of myself.

"Trump shall not be permitted here. What does that sign to your right say," the Being asked? Before the Being spoke it into existence, there was no sign on the cloud to the right. But after asking me the question, a sign emerged from the previously empty cloud and read, "No Democrats or Republicans allowed, only true Independents." Suddenly it all made sense.

Since the Being seemed to be open to answering my questions, I started to fire off countless questions with reckless abandonment as soon as they germinated in the soil of confusion that was my mind.

"We are taught in the beginning there was nothing. If that was the case, how did nothing become something? What created God?" I asked.

"The same thing that created You created God. God created You and You created God," the nonchalant Being with infinite wisdom rapidly replied as if he had stated something that was common knowledge. "Think of it this way, before an idea comes to mind, where does it exist? Nowhere, yet everywhere. An idea is originally nothing, yet it exists somewhere before it's conceived in your mind. An idea can essentially create itself. Now think about that in the context of an infinite universe that has no beginning or ending, a universe that is the Alpha and Omega, a universe that is the great I AM."

Before I could fully digest the Being's answer about what created God, I offered up a question about miracles that I had occasionally pondered. "Miracles like Moses parting the Red Sea and Daniel surviving in the Lion's Den were so prevalent in the past. Why aren't similar miracles possible in today's time?" I inquired.

The Eternal Being moved its hands in a circular motion that I didn't understand and then merged his left index finger and thumb with his right index finger and thumb to create an Ethiopian Pyramid. After making the pyramid, the Eternal One stated, "As time elapses on Earth, man becomes further and further separated from the Creator and universal laws of wisdom. As the pendulum of time swings forward, humans become more fixated on understanding Earth's principles and science while simultaneously losing connection with principles that exist beyond the earthly realm. Keep in mind the universe has many scientific principles that aren't relegated to the five senses of sight, smell, hearing, touch and taste. The more reliant and certain one becomes of the five senses that are understood and widely accepted, the more separated one becomes from the science and knowledge that exists beyond the five conventional senses of Earth. For example, did you know that you and I are currently talking without speaking? As thoughts appear in your mind for you to think or write, so does our conversation. The mind, the spirit and heart are all capable of communicating without words, as cell phones without towers, if you will."

Before the Being mentioned that we were communicating without speaking, I had failed to realize that we were engaging in a full fledge conversation just by thinking our thoughts. As I struggled to keep up with the information that the Being was explaining, I circled back to his initial act of the circular hand motion and the creation of the Ethiopian Pyramid.

"What were you doing when you made the circular motion and created the Ethiopian Pyramid," I asked.

"The first time, I was emulating Dr. Strange from the Avengers movie. I'm a fan of Marvel movies just like you," the Being stated while chuckling.

"This time, I will reveal what is known to me and what is unknown to you. Hidden knowledge that has been lost and buried in the sands of human hate, violence, and complacency."

As the infallible One with no age spoke without speaking, the circular motion and the creation of the Ethiopian Pyramid occurred again, except there was no usage of the Being's hands this time. The Ethiopian Pyramid formed itself out of what appeared to be thin air and hovered between the Being and me. The hieroglyphics on the pyramid lit up and presented an image that looked exactly like the Eternal Being.

The Being continued, "Those before you, the creators of the pyramids, understood and previously interacted with those of us who possess hidden knowledge. The knowledge that I possess has been lost and is not understood by men who build rockets that can traverse space but fail to think or comprehend beyond their five senses."

Before I could even fully digest what the timeless Being had just shown me, I asked one final question.

"What can African Americans do to defeat racism in America?"

The Eternal One took a few moments to think about what I asked and then shared his perspective. "It's simple, the Original Man and Woman love a country that doesn't love them back. When Lucifer and 1/3 of the Angels in heaven decided that they no longer wanted to be here, we helped them leave. Heaven did not fight to remain in a relationship with hate. African Americans have been praying to God for freedom, equality and reconciliation with America for 400 plus years because they refuse to accept the truth that is right in front of them. Hate is not always taught. Sometimes it's a choice. You cannot make a country love something or someone it has chosen to hate at every turn. How long will the Original Man and Woman be adamant about remaining in a one-sided relationship? If too many African Americans move into a particular area, what happens? Choose your desired location and go there in mass numbers. If you flock to an area in mass numbers, those who hate you will move. Destroy and Rebuild.

"Oh yeah, one last point. Something that many don't seem to understand about prayer. Many times, people pray for miracles or God's help unnecessarily. The wisdom and common sense to handle most issues are already within you. If God gave you the tools to solve the problem, why do you need him to solve it for you?"

As I contemplated the information that the ageless One was sharing, I experienced what felt like déjà vu. Suddenly I was in the courtroom, a place that I was most comfortable in. It felt as if I was back on Earth. Perhaps I was reliving or witnessing a memory from my life, or so I thought.

3

HEAVEN MUST BE NICE

I magine being able to erase life with impunity. Imagine being the bad apple that didn't fall far from America's unjust judicial tree. Imagine that you are a paid cop with the licenses to kill people who were previously victims of the Transatlantic Slave Trade, Jim Crow and segregation because America has to remind those who were once slaves that they are still slaves regardless of what the Emancipation Proclamation once declared. Imagine being able to kill with impunity because viewing black people as three-fifths of a human for voting purposes wasn't inhumane enough. Hence, the hate in your heart demands that the Original Man and Woman of Earth must be reduced to zero, reduced to meaning nothing.

Imagine that you are a public servant paid for by tax dollars and entrusted with protecting citizens, but when a person who doesn't share your privileged hue is on the other side of your gun or under your knee, you can freely deprive them of their final breath and never face justice. Imagine being able to take the lives of countless black men and women in perpetuity. Instead of being charged with murder for your vile actions, you are rewarded with administrative leave or awarded paid time off for killing the defenseless. African Americans have never sought revenge, only equality and reconciliation, but we have been met with acts of violence and hate at every turn.

Now, imagine being a black lawyer who defends his people within the confines of the judicial system that has no interest in ever delivering justice for those infused with melanin. This was the fate that I chose when I decided to become a lawyer.

Sometimes I pondered what I would do if I had one bow, one arrow dedicated to justice. Would I fire my lone arrow at the White House to Trump racism? Would I rid the Earth of George Zimmerman and bring peace to the restless soul of Trayvon Martin? Would I choose to zero in on the person I despise most in life, or would I contemplate easing all of life's ills by assassinating myself? Like Freud, I often found myself pondering Id. As Langston Hughes so elegantly stated during the Harlem Renaissance, "Life for me ain't been no crystal stair."

Regarding my life, Langston Hughes' profound words about life failing to be a crystal stair were apropos. No one would ever mistake my ascension from darkness and the climb towards success that has been my life for being beautiful or as easy on the eyes as a crystal stair. Instead, my life was littered with oodles & noodles and marred with dilapidated and unkempt steps that seemed to lead south to hell.

Amid trying to manufacture a compelling defense for one of my best friends, I found myself drifting on a directionless raft towards memories that I longed to bury. My feelings and memories seem to find enjoyment in making me relive the misery of days from my past. I grew up believing in the mantra of, "I'd rather be judged by 12 than carried by 6," that is to say I would rather kill and let a jury decide my fate instead of having my loved ones carry my casket because I let someone kill me first. And I wasn't the only one from the treacherous Tree Port hood that subscribed to this idea. My father believed it; Prince subscribed to it, and everyone else in my crew swore by the same notion, so much so, we lived and died by it daily.

My lifelong best friend was facing eternity for a crime that I couldn't fathom him committing without just cause. With my friend's livelihood and freedom at stake, my mind was ensnared with memories and thoughts from the past. I was trying with all my might to focus on mounting a compelling defense. However, for every second that I tried to spend thinking about how to secure his freedom, my mind would slip further into this dark and haunting, unrelenting sinkhole that was my past.

As a bourgeoning youth in Tree Port, I frequently went without food and occasionally braved the coldest winter nights sans heat. On several occasions, my homework went uncompleted because my family sometimes lived a life without Benjamin Franklin's creation that brightened the world. Being a young boy listening to my mom anxiously pace back and forth when yellow late payment alerts evolved to pink disconnection warnings that ultimately rendered darkness upon our apartment was terrifying. Yellow notices morphing into pink disconnection notices was a rite of passage in my Public Housing development. Each time my family received a new disconnection notice, it was a fresh reminder of how disenfranchised and poor we were. I would silently cry in the dark and share crumbs with nomadic roaches to cope with my despair while wondering why God refused to save those that seemingly needed him the most.

When yellow power bill notices would arrive, my mom would immediately clasp the house phone and make the obligatory phone calls seeking financial help. She tried with all her might to hide our dire financial predicament from my younger brother and me. Her efforts to conceal the perils of failing to defeat darkness were to little avail as the franticness in her voice would carry through the vents of our 2-bedroom abode and gingerly land on the ears of her young sons. My mom would start by calling Big Momma, whom we all knew was broker than broke. My mother was hoping for a miracle. I guess she thought Big Momma might have the money to spare because Big Momma was owed a few blessings from the almighty God in the sky since she religiously paid her ten percent at church. Big Momma was so dedicated to giving the church its ten percent that she would choose tithing before paying past due bills that were piling up on her kitchen countertop. Besides quoting cliché scriptures that would lift my mom's spirit somewhat, Grandma provided little to no financial help most of the time.

After a few minutes of discussing late bills with Grandma, my mom would meticulously move through her remaining contacts. As my mom scrolled through her contacts, she hoped to identify a family member or friend who would offer an entrée of cash without including 'bootstrap rhetoric condemnation' as an accompanying side dish. She would start by calling family members who appeared to be doing better than most. You know the ones who occasionally boasted about how successful they were or tried their best to highlight their ascension to the middle class by creatively mentioning the finer things in life that they had recently discovered. You know the ones that complain about how cheap the vino is at family reunions while simultaneously living paycheck to paycheck themselves. I suppose speaking of wine like a sommelier made individuals in my family feel as if they had eclipsed the poverty and hopelessness of Tree Port for good. I could stomach it somewhat, but I could tell the talk of high-end wine annoyed my mother as she was the type that would have turned down the water that Jesus turned to wine, and she loved herself some Jesus.

Eventually, my mom would work her way through the last of her contacts that could provide no financial assistance, which meant our home's brightness would inch closer and closer to Jesus' hidden and true hue. Eventually, we found ourselves in the same predicament every time, life before God declared, "Let there be light."

As I thought about losing light in my home as a child, the wind beneath the sails of the emotional raft I was stuck on drifted closer and closer to the agony of defeat. As the nightmare of potential defeat grew deeper, memories of my childhood slightly relented as I tried for a second time to focus on the task at hand.

During my most significant court case, I was unprepared. I felt incapable of competently defending my best friend, whom I presumed to be innocent. During my previous eleven trials, not one single time was I unnerved or remotely concerned that any of my clients would land in prison, not even the ones that I knew were guilty. Life is crazy in that way.

The experiences that I thought would prepare me for a moment like this were instead creating rapid heart palpitations and fertilizing seeds of incompetence that could potentially land my ace, my right-hand man, in prison forever. An avalanche of fear entrapped my tongue and entangled my thoughts as I grappled with how to explain why my Tree Port contemporary should be free. Lord knows I would have sacrificed my undefeated record or even thrown a previous case to ensure that my childhood friend would be found innocent of this wicked crime he was accused of. Growing up, I knew I was destined to stand before condescending know-it-alls with gavels one day. Standing before judges and being condemned to dark cells of hopelessness was a rite of passage for many in Tree Port, especially for the underserved and uncared for youth. For a substantial part of my younger years, it felt inevitable that my place of lodging would ultimately switch from public housing to prison. Even my dad was in a prison of his own making, and many of my family members had fallen victim to the entrapment of the prison industrial complex. Just as LeBron was correctly deemed 'a can't miss' NBA prospect, I was forecasted to be the same for Tree Port's prison draft. Judges in our city were hell-bent on doling out maximum sentences to brothers from Tree Port. It didn't matter if the individuals in court were first-time offenders or non-violent and misdemeanor inclined; the max sentence was a train that seemed to never derail for citizens in Tree Port.

In an ill twist of fate that not even my mom, who loved me dearly, could foresee, I never stood in front of a judge to be sentenced. Instead, I became a glimmer of hope for the distressed in Tree Port by becoming an attorney. I don't recall exactly when it occurred, but becoming a lawyer became my destiny. It's not something that I routinely dreamt of in my youth, but somehow, I ended up in court as a renowned and undefeated lawyer taking on the biggest case that one could fathom. Previously, I had managed to defend each of my eleven clients successfully. Several times I foolishly brushed off great plea deals out of sheer ignorance and arrogance before winning cases that seemed to have irrefutable evidence stacked against my clients. Yet, here I was seated next to my close friend of twenty-plus years, melting under what felt like insurmountable pressure during the most critical case of my career. When the volcano of life finally erupts, what happens when the results of immense pressure create cubic zirconia instead of the brilliantly gleaming Hope Diamond?

Coming into my most recent trial, I felt like Muhammad Ali, the Greatest. The more cases I won, the more invincible I felt in the courtroom. Heck, I had been so convincing in the courtroom, I had never even produced a hung jury. But at the moment when it mattered most, with the life of one of my closest friends gingerly dangling in my ill-equipped hands, I felt inadequate. I was desperately grasping at straws and failing to put the pieces of the puzzle together.

As I contemplated the possibility of not being able to free my Tree Port cohort from eternal condemnation, my heart leaped out of my chest. Bullets of sweat danced from the crown of my head and transferred smudges of brown dirt to the collar of my shirt. To compound matters, a headache started to emanate near my temple.

My mind wasn't processing information in the blitzkrieg fashion that I was accustomed to. I couldn't attribute my struggles to beginner anxiety as I had been in far worst predicaments before. Previously, I had consistently mustered up the temerity and strength to take on extremely challenging cases that no sane lawyer would touch. But for some reason, on this occasion, none of that mattered, and I couldn't comprehend why.

During my law school years, we learned early that it was essential to cherry-pick and lean towards only accepting clients whose cases had questionable evidence. That was half the battle in securing a win in court. I repeatedly did the exact opposite. I took on all comers so long as they had the means to afford my services. I took on challenging cases because I didn't fear the judge, prosecutors, or juries that were out to convict my clients. I had no fear. Growing up, I became so accustomed to gunfire that I stopped diving to the floor for cover when shots rang out, so there's no way a judge with just a gavel would ever intimidate me, or so I thought.

During my collegiate years, I remember one of my favorite professors asked the class, what's a winnable case? Hands flew up promptly. The majority of the answers centered on morality, fairness and faith in the potential client's innocence. After twelve or so incorrect answers were rendered by those that excitedly raised their hands, Professor Stone told everybody to put their hands down. Professor Stone walked to the chalkboard and wrote 'Questionable Evidence'. "It doesn't matter what you think or what you feel in your heart. Nor does it matter when a mother proclaiming her child's innocence floods your soul with enough tears to break the levees as Hurricane Katrina did. Her tears should be of no concern to your President Bush sensibilities. A winnable case is a case in which the evidence is poor and questionable at best. By poor, I mean the evidence isn't logical enough for the common woman or man to easily follow. A great lawyer isn't someone who works magic in the courtroom. A great lawyer is someone who knows how to ignore the conniving words and emotions of their potential clients and instead vets the evidence in the same manner that a skeptical or biased jury would. Let that approach guide your decisions when it comes to taking cases."

Professor Stone's words shocked many in the class.

Many of my peers had previously articulated their reasons for deciding to practice defense law. Quite a few of my classmates had decided to pursue becoming defense lawyers because they were hoping to change the world for the better. I didn't go to law school because of some grandiose idealism rooted in saving the world, but I did have the desire to stick it to the system and defending those from Tree Port that could afford my services allowed me to do that. My neighborhood, Tree Port, had produced many legends. Tree Port created legendary trappers, reckless murderers who had become famous for all of the wrong reasons and even Santino Brown. Tino accomplished every kid's dream from our hood when he became the lone person to make it from Tree Port to the NBA. My hood created many things, but it failed to make me a good listener.

Unfortunately, the wise words of wisdom that Professor Stone shared on so many occasions during my collegiate years had fallen on Thomas Edison's ears, as I consistently took on cases where the evidence against my clients was strong. In taking on Prince's case, I had committed the most cardinal sin in criminal defense law. I accepted a case that I was emotional about and inextricably linked to. Life had thrown an innumerable amount of obstacles my way, and on most occasions, I was able to float like a butterfly and sting like Ali. On this day in court, there was no grace of floating like a butterfly, and the punches that I typically delivered with pinpoint accuracy were wildly missing the mark. I couldn't figure out why I was struggling to find my bearings. I had maintained the exact routines that had led me to victory eleven other times. Before any of my cases kicked off, I routinely engaged in mental calisthenics by watching classic Ali fights, or His Airness battle the bad boy Pistons, or old reruns of Perry Mason or Matlock.

Nothing got the wheels in my mind rolling more than analyzing the subtle tendencies, techniques and relentlessness of the greats. The ritual of studying the greats originally started in high school and later materialized strategically during my senior year of college. During high school, Prince, Marcus, Santino and I would watch classic moments like Ali defeating Joe Frazier and Jordan hitting seven three-pointers against the Blazers in the NBA Finals. We even watched Michael Johnson run away from the competition in his dazzling gold shoes during the 1996 Olympics in Atlanta. During my undergrad tenure, the ritual of watching the greats evolved from just enjoying their highs to a quest to understand their lows and why in some instances, even legends came up short in crunch time.

Prince would come to campus draped in the most fly gear, ready to party with Tino and me, only to find me fully engrossed in watching hours of film and reading an inordinate amount of legal literature. Along with reading legal literature, I would devote countless hours to reviewing and understanding renowned philosophical theories offered by the greatest thinkers of the 19th century. Once Prince got settled, he would kick off every visit by encouraging us to pregame before the party to save a penny or two. After successfully conveying the importance of pregaming to save money, Prince would hastily hand Tino and me the most disgusting beer ever, a cheap ice-cold 211 Steel Reserve. I would look at Tino every single time and lament, "Things must be slower than ever in the trap. This peasant needs to learn to cook like he got two stoves to double his profits or something because this disgusting beer, ain't it. Can a brother at least get some tequila, some 1942 Don Julio, perhaps? I better not see Prince buying no Grey Goose for the ladies tonight," I chided. Before continuing to clown with us, Prince would consistently offer the same response as Mitch in *Paid in Full*, "I'm broke baby. Santino and Hassan, y'all know the recession that Reagan orchestrated in the 80s never ended. I'm still recovering from that economic downturn." While Prince wasn't a drug dealer, we always called the various ways he made money a trap because no one knew how he made his money, but people always seemed to fall for him pretending to be cash poor even though he was never really broke or starved for cash.

The only thing worse than the standard silver can 211

Steel Reserves that Prince convinced us to pregame with was the black, red and gold triple export malt liquor edition. As the crew gulped down our 211's, I would eventually get excited and proclaim, "Look at Ali's footwork! Look at how he lured George Foreman in close with the rope-a-dope and waited for the exact right moment to unleash his fury. That's going to be me every time I'm in the courtroom. Prosecutors will be giving me their best shots while I sit there quietly, unbothered. Never objecting when they think I should, just silently jotting notes at the precise moments that the prosecutors deliver what they perceive to be their most inconsequential points. When they deliver what they deem to be their most auspicious and convincing arguments, I'll just sit there unbothered knowing no amount of evidence will ever be enough to convict my clients," I declared.

Tino and Prince would just laugh and provide random commentary while making air quotes, "Ok Matlock, what if your potential client is innocent like OJ and the evidence indicates their likelihood of being convicted is 99 percent homie? You taking that case, Perry Mason? You ain't Johnnie Cochran, homie."

"It doesn't matter," I fired back matter-of-factly. "I don't plan on ever losing a case. Because like Ali, I'm the greatest! I'm a bad man, and the ladies in yawls' lives know it. I'm a bad man, and I'm pretty," I would say as I shuffled my feet like the greatest and threw playful punches that barely missed their respective faces. In many ways watching the greats on film helped me to exude confidence and suppress my worries. At some point, the film-watching ritual devolved into a reliable coping mechanism that allowed me to manage my insecurities. While I successfully managed most of my insecurities, some of them were buried so deep in my soul that they remained blind spots that deep introspection did not detect. Early in my life, I learned that all it took was one false step to make a pivotal mistake that couldn't be undone. I'm not sure when it occurred, but my identity was deeply rooted in the belief that I always had to be there when people needed me the most. At family gatherings, I always found a way to unearth the big joker in dire moments when playing Spades. But this time, during my twelfth case, the card that conquered all books wasn't present on the pages that I was reading. Like an inexperienced magician fiddling in a top hat and praying that the rabbit was there, I was racking my brain for a glimmer of magic, but to no avail. Much to my chagrin, there was no mental dexterity, no charm, or charismatic perspective that could save me today in the courtroom.

Who's the correct God to pray to when you are truly desperate? Is it Amen-Ra, Allah, Yeshua, or some deity that I had yet to be introduced to? Like which one hears and answers prayers, I wondered because that's who I needed "Here and

Now," as the legendary Luther Vandross had crooned. I was contemplating praying for the first time in what felt like eons when I heard an agitated judge decry, "Mr. Johnson, are you going to present your final argument, or are you just going to continue to sit there twirling your pen, sir."

It was at that precise moment that I stopped twirling my customized law office pen and glanced at my best friend, Prince, with gloom in my eyes. The look of despair that I possessed probably shocked him more than Hilary losing the 2016 Presidential Election to a bumbling idiot. The look in my eyes was one of fear and concession. I was going to lose a case for the first time and my best friend was going to go away forever. I've always wondered if what they said was true. Does life flash before our eyes before we meet our demise? While I was pretty confident, I wasn't dying. My life was flashing before my eyes as I struggled to rise from my seat. As I pushed my hands against the elegant table that Prince and I were seated at, the strength and courage that I had accumulated over the years betrayed me. As my efforts to rise from my seat to stand before the judge failed, suddenly everything went matte black.

4

THE DEVIL IN THE SKY

A few months before I was shot and killed by my best friend, I started seeing a psychologist. I was at a place in life where everybody close to me assumed I was as happy as could be. Unbeknownst to those closest to me, I was going through an extreme bout with depression that had me wondering if I would end up like Apollo Creed when his trainer threw in the towel too late. Unlike boxing, my life had no coach affixed in my corner to assess my weariness and throw in the towel as to say, "You know what, Life, I'm stopping this fight. You're beating this individual to a pulp. No more." Instead of having to survive 12 rounds, some days felt like 18 rounds. In many ways, it felt like the small ills of life had accumulated with time to an astounding weight that I was no longer able to bear effectively. Feeling down for a few hours had grown to entire evenings and eventually evolved to days. The sense of not having accomplished my real goals, the disappointment of not being happily married with two kids in tow could no longer be whisked away by a few whiskeys or a Moscow Mule. Shockingly, the sun's brightness and magnificence can occasionally be eclipsed by a moon that pales in comparison. All it takes is the wrong set of problems and bad timing for a sunny life to suddenly go dark.

I knew I was in deep trouble when my mental disposition started impacting my peace at work. In many ways, my law office functioned as a fortress of calmness and solitude. I owned my own business; I didn't have to answer to anyone, and my clients provided so much chaos that I spent little to no time focusing on my problems. I devoted most of my free time to analyzing and understanding the law's nuances and intricacies. Every time I stepped in front of a judge, I made it my mission to amaze and illuminate the courtroom like a supernova passing through the sky at night. Sans the explosion aspect that supernovas are known for, of course.

My thinking was that if I immersed myself so deeply in my craft and becoming the best lawyer possible that depression would have no sanctuary in my life. Instead, the opposite occurred. The more time I spent in my office, working late nights and early mornings, the more alone I felt. Success and money failed to become the beautiful companions that I imagined them to be during my poverty-stricken youth.

My place of solitude, my workplace, my perfect safe zone

was no longer safe. My once decadent and peaceful palace was flooded with despair and hopelessness. I was struggling to tread water once the iceberg of depression crashed into my titanic castle. I was quickly annoyed by potential clients. I was missing mentoring sessions with the youth at the Tree Port Community Center and ignoring the woman closest to me. I was sinking.

One day as I sat in my office ignoring calls while playing chess one on one with myself, I concluded that it would be beneficial to talk to someone. It was scary realizing I had issues that I couldn't think through or self-medicate away. My solution to everything was to think and stress more until a solution that I hadn't thought of before becomes apparent. I always felt like maintaining a decent amount of pressure helped to fuel me, but over time, my stress managed to marry my problems and eventually divorced me from happiness.

Is there a person that a black man in America can turn to in confidence when he's struggling to navigate the pressure and pain that comes with being the Original Man that is lost in a land that he doesn't belong in? Can a black man safely confide in anyone when the constant unjustified violence that America perpetrates against him and those who look just like him pushes him to the edge; when he's tired of seeing unarmed brothers and sisters being murdered in the streets by cops? Is there a voice that is willing to remain silent long enough to listen to his concerns for once? Is there a haven of any sort for a broken black man when he feels unloved and realizes that his life doesn't matter in the purported land of the free? Is there a person or institution that a black man in America can turn to when his prayers and silent cries for help go unanswered? Is there a shoulder that a black man can lean on, shed tears on without being deemed weak? Is there an ear that will listen and hear the pain that emerges from the blue blood in our veins that turns red when the bullets from cops ravish our skin and shatter our hopes and dreams while confirming that our lives don't matter? Is there any place on Earth that protects and cares about black men? Is there a present-day Aksum, a kingdom for us and our greatness to exist in peace? That, I do not know.

I sat in silence while pondering the pros and cons of seeking professional help. One of the pros was that I would have an experienced expert who would supposedly listen to my issues without judging me and deeming me weak. The cons were that I would be sharing my fears and secrets with a complete and total stranger that might not understand my plight or way of thinking. I would be sharing the intimate details of my life with a person who might misinterpret the trauma that I had fought hard to survive. After weighing the pros and cons of seeking help, I eventually mustered up the courage to pursue seeing a professional regarding my deteriorating mental state. I decided that a well-respected psychologist would serve me best.

After coming to terms with the need for professional help, I contacted a renowned psychologist named Dr. Jessica Williams. A few telephone conversations occurred before I convinced Dr. Williams it was in my best interest to not meet at her office for my sessions. Without divulging the real reason for my extreme discreetness, I was able to leverage the public figure aspect of my career to bring her on board with my approach. My request for extreme privacy was driven by embarrassment and sheer ignorance about mental health at the time. A small part of me knew that seeking treatment for mental health issues was no different than seeking treatment for a physical ailment, but early on in the process, the stigma or possibility of being called crazy drove me to be hyper-vigilant in ensuring that no one knew my mental health was on the fritz. To hide the embarrassment I felt when meeting with my psychologist and to eliminate the risk of someone discovering that I saw one, I asked Dr. Jessica Williams if she would be willing to conduct our sessions at my home office. Eventually, she came on board with my preferred approach and our sessions began.

My quaint condo was nestled in the left corner of a cul-de-sac in a pleasant and diverse neighborhood that my excellent realtor Renardo Kennedy helped me to secure for purchase. Within the confines of my home, I turned my decently sized loft into a makeshift home office that also doubled as my man cave. While waiting for Dr. Williams to show up for our first in-home session, I rocked back and forth slowly in a silver office chair that had just enough bend without fully reclining. Various thoughts and emotions ran through my mind as I looked at what I deemed the Wall of Admiration. My Wall of Admiration was located to the left of where I was sitting. It consisted of rare black and white photos of individuals I admired deeply. Including legends such as Patrice Lumumba, Medgar Evers, Colin Kaepernick, Shirley Chisolm, Malcolm X, Martin Luther King, LeBron James, Madam CJ Walker, Nas and Bob Marley, to name a few.

As I was sitting and reminiscing, I heard that same loud rhythmic knock that the police used to deliver during my young years. Most of the time, the jakes executed no-knock warrants and kicked the door in without knocking, but in some rare instances, they delivered that same rhythmic knock that the good doctor was delivering. Even though I knew it was Dr. Williams knocking, her police knock still managed to trigger me occasionally. When she would knock, I would sometimes make a startling forward lunge from my chair. My right foot would automatically angle towards the nearest exit as if I were about to run out the back door and scale the nearest fence to evade the racist police officer chasing me. In this scenario running to the nearest exit would be silly as I was currently on the second floor of my condo, which would make the nearest exit a 2nd story window. A second or two later, I calmed down and briskly walked towards the door to welcome Dr. Williams into my home.

Dr. Williams stood about five-eight and always arrived wearing a scent that eluded my in-depth knowledge of perfumes. Every time she came, our greeting was the same, never a hug, always a handshake and hello. We would then head to my office and pick a Chianti from my wine rack to enjoy. During our first session, I poured a glass of wine just for myself as I assumed that it was unethical for a psychologist to drink during a session. To my astonishment, a perplexed Dr. Williams inquired, "Where's my glass?" Not one to upset someone who was doing me a favor, I quickly obliged by grabbing an additional glass and attempted to pour her a drink. As I was preparing to pour, she promptly requested the bottle and noted, "I always pour my own wine." Once our strange wine tango came to an end, we took our seats and kicked off our discussion.

I have no idea why I was so comfortable sharing my innermost thoughts and fears with a person who essentially was a stranger. In addition to being a stranger, she was a liberal from up north who felt America was managing race relations better than it really was. At times, our supposed white liberal allies and bourgeoisie black people drove me crazy with their optimistic views. The views they espoused were often centered around the notion that all we needed was more unity and love to defeat systemic oppression. Our purported allies never mentioned why reparations are required to combat the centuries of systemic oppression that have dug a hole so deep for black people that we are eye to eye with the Devil in hell. I had grown tired of the kumbaya rhetoric and appeasement that our allies repeatedly offered in response to racism. I had grown weary and frustrated with seeing NFL players locking arms before games as a sign of unity to counteract Colin's powerful stance of kneeling. I had tremendous respect for Colin Kaepernick and Eric Reid, and in support of their efforts, I had boycotted the NFL for several years and had no plans of ever watching again.

My very first meeting with Dr. Williams occurred a few weeks after slumlord Trump won the presidential election. As expected, when something sends shockwaves throughout the world, it inevitably becomes a topic of discussion no matter the setting or forum. My meeting with my newly acquired psychologist started with her asking me to share a little about myself. I tactfully mentioned mostly positives such as graduating from undergrad, earning my J.D. degree from law school and mentoring the youth at the Tree Port Community Center. Suddenly, my rundown of the positive aspects of my life and career transitioned to a political conversation. At some point during our conversation, I shared my disdain for those who voted for Trump under the racially motivated ruse of making America great again. After listening to me denounce the American people for a few minutes, Dr. Williams interjected with, "Although Democrats lost the election, we can't make assumptions about the people who voted for Trump. They're not all racists or sexists; most are working middle-class Americans who want to make America great again." *The Make America Great Again* motto made my skin crawl every time I heard it uttered. For more than 400 years, America had failed to live up to its core tenant and promise of treating all people equally, and it had never been great for black people.

"First of all," I lamented. "When people say *Make America Great Again,* they need to explain who it was once great for and acknowledge that by in large the greatness that they feel has disappeared is intrinsically linked to the oppression of others. It's a statement that embodies the quest of many to rollback political and social justice advancements that seek to create equality across race, gender, income disparities and a litany of categories that people use to oppress and divide others."

She let out a long sigh, lifted her glass and then put it back down without taking a sip before stating, "I don't think they want to revert to the Jim Crow era. They want their financial concerns and preferred societal norms to be weighed fairly."

"See, this is my problem with our supposed white liberal allies such as yourself. Do you see how eager you are to understand the concerns of the white working and middle classes? Where's that same concern and desire to understand that same segment of black people who also belong to the working and middle classes? We have voted overwhelmingly for Democrats for decades, only to be rewarded with an occasional symbolic victory and no other substantial material gains." I angrily stated.

"Ms. Williams, have you ever heard of Dr. Claud Anderson?" I asked.

"Can't say that I have," she replied.

"Well, one of his primary arguments for black empowerment is rooted in economics. He explains how wealth for the black community hasn't grown much from the 1900s to today. Suppose America is truly the beacon of freedom and opportunity that people believe it to be. Why has systemic racism been able to prevent black wealth from growing even a scintilla in this vast economy when compared to black wealth in the early 1900s? That's how powerful systemic oppression is. Racism is so powerful that it's undefeated. Even the greatest Muhammad Ali took a loss occasionally, but racism has yet to experience a significant loss of any sort. It's been undefeated since my ancestors were snatched from the Motherland and shackled on those murderous ships. Systemic oppression is a parasite that metastasizes and morphs as needed to prevent hard-working blacks and college-educated blacks from getting a piece of the pie. Heck, how many banks have been in the news lately for predatory and unfair lending when it comes to minorities? It's no different than the redlining and refusal to grant minorities who fought in World War II and the Vietnam War housing loans and then magically finding a way to blame the oppressed group for not owning houses or closing the wealth gap."

A noticeably flustered Dr. Williams took a deep breath, lifted her wine glass, only to set it back down again without taking a sip before saying, "duly noted Hassan, duly noted. Let's redirect our focus from society's ills and discuss the happenings of your life. So, you're preparing for the biggest case of your life this week, correct?" She inquired.

"Something like that," I replied. At that moment, Dr. Williams was able to detect that my aura of invincibility was dissipating rapidly. She probed further, "How do you feel about your chances of winning this case? Why are you so afraid of losing?"

"How can I be afraid of something that's never happened and that will never occur so long as I'm upright and breathing?" I retorted while attempting to convey supreme confidence. "There's no possible way I'll lose the most significant case of my life. I won't let it happen," I continued as I reached for my glass. "But you have experienced defeat before, correct? Let us not strike the loss you took in high school from the history books, Mr. Johnson. That Tree Port High basketball team that you and your friend Santino led to the semifinals during your junior year loss to West End, right?" Triggered by a memory that I had long buried, I quickly recovered from her sharp verbal jab. "That was a loss in a team sport, and it isn't comparable to what you are projecting as an imminent individual loss," I defensively retorted.

Not to be outmaneuvered by my Ali-like feet shuffling dance tactics, Dr. Williams absorbed the uppercut I succinctly delivered and replied, "Mr. Johnson, I never said you would lose your upcoming case. Additionally, the loss you took in high school can be juxtaposed with a first-time loss in the courtroom. Basketball is, without a doubt, a team sport where multiple players contribute to wins and losses, as is the courtroom. Don't forget, each legal victory you secure is an even bigger win for the individuals who avert prison and their families. Some wins and losses can and should be viewed as both individual and team results, indubitably."

Dr. Williams' insight enlightened me about something that I hadn't considered. Before hearing her perspective regarding wins and losses, I failed to grasp that what I accomplished in the courtroom went beyond my aspirations and agenda. Sure, I cared about my clients and their families' general well-being, but I was mostly driven by my desire to never experience another loss. I was using my courtroom victories as a coping mechanism to deal with a loss in my personal life that prevented me from fully respecting and appreciating the fragility of holding others' lives and freedom in my hands. I just knew that losing felt awful and I never wanted to experience it again. The blow that Dr. Williams delivered while analyzing my insecurities felt like the blow that Frazier landed to knock Ali out. I had no response; I was out cold. I was at a loss for words. As Dr. Williams' words sunk deeper into my conscious, I thought about how I was holding my latest client's life and his family's future in my hands. I was preoccupied with maintaining an unblemished record when I should have been focusing on securing my client's freedom.

As my newly discovered epiphany started to sink in further, Dr. Williams stood up and said, "Well, Hassan, our time has expired. Let's meet again next week." As I rose from my seat, I noticed that Dr. Williams hadn't touched her wine at all. Upon exiting the loft area and heading towards the steps, I wondered what type of uncivilized person pours themselves an expensive glass of wine and then forgets to drink it.

After Dr. Williams made her exit, I crept towards my

window and gingerly lifted a few of my blinds' eyelids. My eyes pierced discretely through the night's darkness to ensure she made it to her car safely. I noticed that she had one-upped me on the car front. The good doctor drove an Audi R8 while I wheeled an Audi R7. As if having a better car didn't rev my insatiable capitalistic desires enough, her expensive glittering rims managed to taunt my insufficient fund pockets as she sped off into the darkness of night. As I moseyed back to my seat, I thought about drinking Dr. Williams' untouched glass of wine. Ultimately, my better senses dismissed another round of wine in favor of Uncle Nearest 1856. I needed something more substantial than wine to cope with the unsettling reality that a complete stranger had navigated the complicated landmine that was typically my silent unabated thoughts.

Before meeting with the good doctor, I was petrified. Now that I was officially seeing a psychologist, my initial trepidation had morphed into full-fledged paranoia. I was on the precipice of self-diagnosing myself as crazy. Does talking to someone about your deepest feelings mean you are unstable or on the verge of psychosis, or do suicidal thoughts have to follow first, I pondered? I had defended many clients and even dated a young lady who consistently met with a therapist. I didn't view my past clients or former girlfriend who met with therapists as crazy. Their situations were akin to seeing a doctor for a physical ailment to me, but now that I was seeking solace for my receding mental state, it felt incredibly awkward. Never would I have imagined that my adulthood problems would dwarf the traumas of growing up in Tree Port. I had survived countless shootouts, survived poverty that saw me curse the crumbs that unintentionally escaped my hands and fell to the roaches, all while enduring a litany of unfortunate events. Yet, here I was as an educated, well-paid adult willing to discuss my problems with a psychologist. "I'm not crazy," I muttered as I stared at my reflection as it danced off the lightly tinted green glass that sheltered my drink. As my thoughts shifted from analyzing what exactly constitutes one being crazy, I reached for my liquid safety net.

I knocked back my generous pour of Uncle Nearest in record time. I slowly sunk into my couch as if I were seeking to become intertwined with the splashes of gold scattered throughout it. No sooner than two minutes after resting my empty glass on the end-table closest to my seat, my eyelids started to flutter. After a few more flutters, the light in the room drew nigh and flickered for the final time as my eyes slammed shut. As I dozed off, I dreamt of difficult times from my youth that I had retroactively romanticized as being simple.

There I was surrounded by my crew just like old times. Santino appeared out of nowhere and dribbled his favorite basketball with skills that the rest of us envied. Santino was so nice with the rock that he reminded us of a young Bubba Chuck, aka Allen Iverson. He had crazy handles that made it look like he was dancing with his shadow when he dribbled and a jumper that was nothing but net after leaving his hands. His longtime sweetheart and future wife Candace was on the sideline, admiring every shot that floated from his hand to the tattered rim draped with a silver chain net.

My lifelong friend Prince was also in the building chopping it up with Santino's older brother Shawn. Shawn would later catch a long bid for attempted murder that ended his appearances at the blacktop. Prince was busy being Prince, the center of attention, the one giving the Nothing to Lose crew unsolicited words of wisdom to live by. To Prince and Shawn's right was my seven-thirty crazy cousin Marcus and one of my best friends Tasha or Tee as I affectionately called her. As the familiar faces that were routinely at the legendary blacktop court floated by, my memory suddenly jolted me back to a different time, a dreadful day that none of us would ever forget.

On most days, I walked to the court without my younger brother or at least caught a ride in a car with tinted windows, but on that fateful day, I decided it was okay for my younger brother Deuce to tag along with me. So many times, Deuce had begged me to take him to the basketball court. "Hassan, come on, let me go this time, pretty please. I promise I'll be good," he pleaded on each occasion as I would get dressed before heading to the blacktop. "Not today Deuce, next time," I would reply every time as I patted him on the head. Immediately after, I would say, "Not today Deuce, next time," Deuce would dive on his bed, bury his face into his pillow and begin to kick and cry. As much as I would have loved to have taken my brother Deuce to the blacktop court, it wasn't safe for him to go. For some strange reason, on that particular day, I responded differently. I tossed my deep apprehension regarding his safety to the side.

When he asked if he could roll to the court with me, I just said, "put on your shoes." An excited Deuce quickly grabbed his Nikes and laced them as if he would be the first player selected when we reached the court. "I finally get to see my idol Tino ball out," he exclaimed." Deuce was like every young child in Tree Port, the biggest fan of Santino and his skills on the court. Secretly it was my wish that Deuce would one day admire me the way he looked up to Santino. Whenever word got out that Santino would be hooping on a particular day, the young kids in the hood would beg and plead with their parents and older siblings about going to the basketball court to witness the magical experience of Santino playing ball.

After I let Deuce know that he could finally roll to the court with me, he became so filled with excitement that he bounced back and forth across the room as I called Tee to see if she could give us a ride to the blacktop.

"Hassan, what's good?" she asked after answering my call after the third ring.

"Tee, what's good? Can you do your boy a major quick favor? Can you come get Deuce and me and drop us off at the court?"

"Man, I wish you would have hit me up earlier, Hassan. I can't come to get you and Deuce right now because I'm already at the court. I rode with Keisha. I can't believe you're bringing Deuce to the court with you, you sure that's a good move? As a matter of fact, let me see if I can talk the fellas into coming to get you."

I paused for a few moments as I contemplated Tee's question, which was rooted in justified concern. "Tee, it's all good. We will be safe. We should see you in the next twenty minutes or so," I stated as my call with Tee concluded.

Since Tee couldn't chauffer Deuce and me to the court, I reviewed the safety protocol with Deuce to ensure he was on point before leaving the house.

"Deuce, what're the rules we follow when leaving the house?"

An excited Deuce quickly recited the safety protocol that I had drilled into his head a thousand times before.

"Keep my head on a swivel at all times! Alert you

immediately if I see anyone suspicious eyeing us or any cars creeping by at reduced speeds. For four minutes, walk as fast as possible and then turn right on St. James to avoid the alleyway on Dawson Way. After turning right on St. James, I jog to Ms. Tina's yard, pivot left and then walk straight with my head below the privacy fences for three minutes. Once we reach Dupoint Ave, look left and right to see if any unknown cars are occupied and parked on the street before keeping straight. If any unknown cars are occupied, wait for the driver to either drive off or exit the vehicle and enter a house before keeping straight to cross the street. Start jogging until Dupoint turns into Fairview and we reach the court safely."

I proudly smiled as Deuce recanted all the safety protocols without missing a beat and gave him a pound.

"Oh yeah, if for some reason something bad happens to me, what do you know about your big brother?"

"I know my big brother is proud of me and loves me very much," Deuce stated as he ran towards me and gave me a jubilant hug.

"Big facts. Major facts only. Your big brother loves you to death forever." I stated as we embraced.

As our embrace concluded, Deuce inquired about something that my crew and I had contemplated for many years. The million-dollar question that we had no real answer for. "Hassan, why do people in Tree Port want to kill us?"

Hearing my nine-year-old brother ask and contemplate such a heavy and complicated question broke my heart. My younger brother should have been focused on learning his multiplications, playing with new toys and enjoying life as a little child. Instead, he was inquiring about the harsh realities of Tree Port's street politics. That was the reality of life in Tree Port. Young kids had to live their lives wondering why our block hated this block, why this block had animosity towards our block and why this hood had static with that hood.

When my mom and dad brought my younger brother home from Tree Port Memorial Hospital after his birth, my top priority and life mission became protecting him at all cost. Many nights I heard my mom praying, "Dear heavenly Father, I come to you humbly, seeking your protection for my two sons, Hassan and Deuce. Protect them as they go to and fro. Give them the wisdom needed to navigate these dangerous blocks. Give my husband and me the ability to secure their futures and the ability to give them a better tomorrow. In your precious and holy name, I pray," she would say. Sometimes after her prayer, my father would try to reassure her that we would be ok. "Michelle, I'm not telling you not to pray, but prayers don't come with bullets. If praying makes you feel better, then, by all means, pray. Just remember, the gun that I gave Hassan and the gun that I will give Deuce when he's old enough will protect them in these streets, not God. Have you seen how many bullets God has turned a blind eye to when it comes to little children in our streets? I don't think America or God cares about our kids," he would state as my mom most likely turned her back and rolled over to ignore him while silently saying a few more prayers regarding our safety.

The blocks and politics of Tree Port weren't for the faint of heart. Teaching Deuce the truth about life where we resided was paramount to his safety, but I had no honest answer in this instance. I didn't know the real reason why the West End despised my block so much, and I didn't know the origin of why my block hated the West End so much. I just knew they hated us and we hated them.

As I pondered Deuce's inquiry about why the West End hated us, I inhaled deeply and released my frustration with a quiet sigh. Perturbed by my silence and refusal to answer, Deuce slightly altered his probe and pressed again, "Hassan, why are there people who want to kill me?" Having no response that would placate my younger brother, I begrudgingly replied, "Deuce, they just do. It's like how America has been out to destroy and kill black people for four hundred years, even though we don't know why they want to kill us so badly. All you need to know is that it doesn't matter what the West End wants to do because I won't ever let them do it."

After we finished discussing the unknown factors that

drove Tree Port's residents to the genocidal intersections of death and hate, Deuce and I headed out the back door. After exiting the house, we hastily started our trek to the legendary blacktop court. Deuce was more anxious than I was. He couldn't wait to see Santino deliver his Earl 'The Pearl' Monroe moves up close and personal. While walking, I reiterated to Deuce that he needed to alert me immediately if he noticed anyone suspicious eyeing us or any cars driving by at reduced speeds while we were walking. Although Tree Port was in a time of peace, it was imperative to remain vigilant and on point at all times as certain neighborhoods refused to adhere to the peace treaties that all sides had "agreed" to. Our hood was so dangerous that we only traveled in vehicles with tinted windows. If we had to step foot in a car with no tint for some reason, it was a requirement that we wear a hoody to hide our face and recline the passenger seat all the way back to avoid being seen by an enemy that wanted to harm us. Wearing a hoody during eighty and ninety-degree weather was absurd, but it was one of the only ways to remain anonymous and safe. In addition to wearing hoodies during the warmest part of summer, there was no waiting outside at the bus stop to catch the bus for school as that made us sitting ducks for a potential drive-by.

Under normal circumstances, no one in our crew would walk to the basketball court without at least another crew member or at the very least a fully loaded pistol. Nevertheless, there I was, walking to the court with the person who mattered most to me without my friends watching my back and no gun. Tree Port was a dangerous maze that even my mom, who had no firm ties to the streets, had to learn to navigate when violence was at its apex.

Whenever my mother arrived home, she had to look over her shoulder to make sure no enemies were lying in wait in unknown vehicles to cause her harm. Because she was from our block, she had to take extra precautions that law-abiding citizens shouldn't be burdened with.

Once Deuce and I safely neared our destination, I exhaled a huge sigh of relief as the blacktop and shadows of members from the Nothing to Lose crew climbed from beyond the horizon and grew closer.

When Deuce and I neared the court, I spotted my cousin Tory in his silver jeep. Santino was joking with Tory about how his little son knew all the words to the album Forest Hill Drive because Tory bumped Fayetteville's own, J. Cole, all the time. As Santino was nodding his head and catching the vibe, I heard Tory say, "I'm telling you Young Simba is the best rapper from this generation, whatever 'It' is he got 'It.' A true artist for the people." Hearing my cousin make that proclamation was fascinating. His favorite rappers were Rakim, Nas, Biggie, Wale and now apparently J Cole. Tory didn't come to the court frequently, but he always went out of his way to show up and provide an extra set of eyes whenever word spread that Santino was playing. Tory and many others from our hood and surrounding blocks that were our allies felt immense pressure to protect Tino as he was the hood's hope. As Tory and Santino continued their conversation about music and dope lyricists, Esco's legendary lyrics depicting the options of freedom or jail and detailing how murder occurs at the same time a man is born blared from the speaker as Deuce and I reached the entrance of the blacktop.

Upon arriving, I surveyed the court and removed the latch to the rusting silver gate that surrounded the blacktop. As Deuce looked on in awe and admiration, I approached the Nothing to Lose crew. I greeted everybody one by one with our unique, complicated handshakes. As I completed my final handshake with the rocket blasting off finale, Prince informed me that the crew had called next.

"Oh yeah, bruh, you gotta sit this one out. A serf took your spot since you took forever to get here," Prince nonchalantly stated as he lifted Deuce towards the sky and hugged him while saying, "Deuce, I love you. I'm glad your brother finally let you come to the court to see us play ball."

As Prince's shenanigans with Deuce concluded, I quipped, "It's like that? I arrive on standard CP time, just fifteen minutes late and this the thanks I get? I hope y'all lose,"

I jokingly chided.

As Prince made a beeline towards the court, he made his final proclamation, "Just call next H, but of course none of us will be on your squad because we about to run the table on these suckers!"

The Nothing to Lose ensemble chimed in with a chorus of laughter because they knew having Tino on their team guaranteed that they would run the table. That also meant that I would be taking an L in the next game if I called next. Since I was no fool, I decided not to call next and instead plopped down in my cousin's former place of rest and proceeded to greet Tee. Tee stood approximately five-four, about four inches shorter than me. Her gorgeous smile complimented her pleasant personality well and lit up any room that she stepped foot in. My crew and her friends frequently inquired about us just being friends. I suppose those closest to us detected some sort of romantic chemistry that was dormant to us. We never shared a kiss, never danced at the school dances, or even held hands during grade school. And on most occasions, we greeted each other with the non-sensual hugs that disinterested women loved to deliver to parishioners at church. She was indeed just one of my best friends, and I loved her as such. I was astonished that none of the snipers from the NTL crew never shot their shot with Tee. She was fine, funny and extremely intelligent. What more could a person want or desire in a girlfriend? Occasionally whenever Tee and I were in the same place as Santino, he would pull me to the side and ask, "Hassan, what's the holdup? She's not going to wait forever, you know."

I was so deeply engulfed in my conversation with Tee; I paid little to no mind to the happenings on the court. Why would I? I had seen this movie play out numerous times. The opposing team always put their best foot forward only to see Tino take over the game late and run them off the court. At some point, I heard things get pretty contentious, and the increasing decibels of the angry voices became more noticeable. Such commotion at the blacktop court in Tree Port was relatively common, so Tee and I paid the loud bickering between the teams on the court no mind. We continued to talk about everything under the sun. Topics ranged from the upcoming basketball season, the first black president and this book she was reading called My Refusal. Right when she asked if I would be the 6th man or crack the starting lineup for our high school team, multiple gunshots shattered our conversation and silenced the loud voices playing ball. My protective instincts took over, and I immediately jumped on top of Tee to cover and shield her from any deadly bullets that might have our names on them. While I was on top of Tee, I closed my eyes tightly as I waited for the dreadful gunshots to cease. Once the shots stopped ringing, I rolled off of Tee. As a flood of tears streamed down her face, she wailed in deep fear and concern, "Hassan, you good, you good?" As she patted my stomach and back to ensure I wasn't hit. "Tee, I'm good, chill, chill," I retorted as I surveyed the landscape to ensure the shooters weren't reloading. As I struggled to gain my bearings, my heart sunk lower than the ocean floor because I remembered that I had given my younger brother Deuce permission to come to the court with me. I immediately panicked, "Tee, I can't believe I let Deuce out of my sight. We gotta find him now!" I yelled.

It was pure mayhem. Discombobulated people with tears running down their faces were screaming while franticly searching the blacktop to see if their family members or friends had been shot. As my panic meter reached its apex, Tee and I noticed a crowd gravitating towards the other end of the court. An older lady named Ms. Nichols that lived near the basketball court, consistently came to watch the games and sell 25 cent popsicles. She was such a thoughtful and kind spirit. Ms. Nichols graciously gave free popsicles to the kids that couldn't afford to pay while smiling and saying, "It's okay, darling, just pay me the next time I see you." Instead of passing out popsicles, she was imploring everyone around to call 911. "Call 911, call 911, or this little boy is going to die," she exclaimed. Horror and hopelessness gripped my heart as Tee and I anxiously made our way towards the crowd surrounding the little boy who had been shot.

I hadn't ventured to church with my mom or Big Momma in forever, but the one thing that came to mind at that moment was praying. Tears welled in my eyes, but not one fell as I prayed, God, please don't let my brother die, please don't let my brother die. Tee's deeply rooted faith in God was unshaken by the mayhem. I could make out her saying a plea that was deliberate and thoughtful to the Almighty. As we approached and got close enough to see the body sprawled on the warm concrete, I closed my eyes and clenched Tee's hand tightly. While my eyes were closed, I thought I heard an Angel declare, "it's not Deuce." As I quickly snapped out of my daze, I heard the Angel say, "it's not Deuce," again.

Once I opened my eyes, I realized it wasn't archangel Gabriel speaking. It was Tee. "Hassan, it's not Deuce," she whispered as she hugged me tightly. Lying on the ground was a different 9- year-old boy from Tree Port. Tee nor I knew the little boy, but we cried confused tears of sadness and joy as he gasped for air. As we shuffled away from the crowd, we finally heard the arrival of ambulance sirens. The paramedics made a quick exit from their vehicle and swiftly unloaded the gurney. The woman that sold popsicles cried out, "it's too late. He's not breathing."

We stood back as the paramedics applied pressure to the

young boy's wound and administered CPR. "One, two, three, breathe," the paramedics repeated the saying over and over again for several minutes as they breathed air into his mouth and pushed on the boy's chest as they pleaded for him to come back to life. It was too late. The young boy refused to emulate Jesus. He didn't rise again and there would be no Resurrection Sunday in his honor. Just that quick, a basketball game had devolved into violence that saw Tree Port incur its first homicide in a long while.

During all the madness, Tee and I had still failed to locate Deuce. As we scanned from side to side, we eventually saw Prince walking towards us with Deuce in tow. I don't even know if I believed in miracles, but this certainly felt like the closest thing to one. An out of breath, Prince explained, "Once I heard the shots go off, I immediately ran to get Deuce." I was at a loss for words. I immediately clutched my best friend and began to cry. No one had ever seen me cry before except Tee, but I couldn't hold my tears of profound thankfulness back. Tee hugged Deuce, picked him up and spun him around as she passionately kissed him on the cheek.

I don't think Deuce fully comprehended the madness or the act of violence that transpired. Deuce was accustomed to me being overprotective because my mother and I made it our top priority to insulate Deuce from the dark tumultuous clouds that rained drops of pain, hopelessness and despair on the residents of Tree Port.

Once Tee stopped spinning Deuce around, I told him I love you repeatedly while I patted his head incessantly. My number one goal in life was protecting my brother at all costs, even if that required shooting first and asking questions later. Deuce's safety came before my schoolwork and my high school basketball quest of cracking the starting lineup to star alongside Tino. Amid my wonderful reunion with Deuce, Prince asked, "Did the other little boy live?" At a loss for words, Tee and I just shook our heads as we struggled to find the appropriate thoughts to break the bad news to Prince. Sheer disappointment and heartache gripped Prince's face. At that moment, I saw the Prince I had known for so many years start his evolution of becoming a more pragmatic person that believed *By Any Means Necessary*. His core attributes of being analytical, decisive and caring for those closest to him remained, but his faith in people was greatly diminished when that 9-year-old boy took his final and last breath. Prince paced back and forth for a few minutes as if he were contemplating what he could have done differently to prevent the young boy from losing his life. "Never again," he uttered as he wandered into the darkness without even telling me, Deuce, or Tee peace.

As Prince and his newfound best friend of despair dissolved into the darkness of the night, I heard my cousin

Tory approach. "H and Tee, y'all good," he asked as he gave me a pound and hug. While we embraced, Tory patted me down like an overzealous beat cop searching for drugs to ensure my adrenaline wasn't protecting me from a bullet wound that I was unaware of. "Yo Hassan, do me a favor. If you or your mom talk to my wife, don't let her know I was here." Before I could respond, Tory assumed I was on board with his request and disappeared into the night with his young son in tow.

5

FOOLISH WISDOM

T he death of that 9-year-old significantly altered the street politics of Tree Port. An onslaught of violence between my neighborhood and the West End produced fatalities and many gunshots wound victims. Before the war with the West End kicked off, the Nothing to Lose crew was vehemently opposed to violence. In large part, that could be attributed to Prince's desire to keep the peace. Refraining from harming anybody Black unless it was completely necessary was something, he was adamant about. I never opposed violence completely, as violence and death were intrinsically linked to getting things accomplished in America. In my estimation, America isn't the land of the free. It's the land of kill or be killed. America is the soil that has been drenched by the blood of the oppressed to produce wealth for those that espouse the virtues of capitalism and hyper-consumerism. All in the name of enriching themselves further, no matter the overall detriment to society. It's a country filled with citizens who love their guns and bullets more than they love the God who commanded us to love thy neighbor as thyself. I suppose some people value their hate for others more than they value the idea of eternal life in heaven.

I vividly recall an incident where someone from the West End mistakenly shot a grandmother from Tree Port, and Prince still adamantly refusing to respond with violence. "I don't go to bed at night and purposely dream about murder, but sometimes my nightmares have a mind of their own. Violence isn't my preference, but I'm not opposed to it," I told the crew as I brandished my silver semi-automatic handgun. "I'm not afraid to confront hate. Tell me where the hate is so I can sprint towards it and eradicate it. So, you mean to tell me, we just gonna sit back and let those clowns from the West End shoot innocent grandmas that are carrying groceries into their apartments," I asked as I looked at my friends with disgust and disappointment.

Outside of Marcus, no one in the crew backed my resolution of going to war. As I assessed the energy of my comrades, I tried one final hail-Mary. "Prince, this is your Toussaint L'Ouverture moment. It's Haiti versus France! We need to end this now before it gets out of hand. There is no freedom without sacrifice!" I exclaimed. "Let's end this war once and for all," I declared. "If we don't kill them, they will kill us. We can choose to stand on business and protect those most vulnerable, or we can end up annexed like Poland during World War II. It's only so much ground you can concede before you end up like Switzerland." My enthusiasm for war and insatiable desire to end the beef with the West End once and for all fell on Van Gogh's missing ear. My ominous warning was unheard. Instead, we offered appeasement just like the countries that would later end up annexed during World War II. It's not realistic or safe to be Switzerland or Poland in the hood. You better pick up a gun or end up dead, I thought to myself once I realized that the Nothing to Lose crew was choosing defeat over victory.

While that grandmother getting shot didn't cause much movement in our hood, that 9-year-old getting killed did the opposite. His death prompted the powers that be in Tree Port to come together for a meeting of the minds. In my opinion, these meetings were useless, but for some reason, Prince asked me to tag along for this one. Prince was deferential and advocated peace during the meeting but was still met with animus from the West End leader. As I grew increasingly frustrated with Renlo, the knucklehead leader of the West End regime, I pulled my pistol when he denied that the bullet that erased the 9-year-old's life didn't come from his crew for the third time. After pulling my gun out, I pointed it directly at Renlo's head. With my weapon drawn and pointed at Renlo's head, I stated, "Your crew specializes in robbing the elderly, disrespecting the defenseless and shooting innocent people with no remorse. That child who died could have been my little brother Deuce. I should blow your brains out right now." The whole time that I had my pistol pointed at the West End leader, he didn't break a sweat or even offer blinks of panic. It was as if Renlo had no soul or fear. He just cracked a devilish grin while nodding his head as he dared me to pull the trigger. He didn't fear me, and he didn't fear death. Sensing that I had made a critical mistake, Prince quickly intervened. As I contemplated divorcing Renlo's soul from life, Prince pushed my hand down, which lowered the gun barrel that was reflecting in Renlo's eyes. I had missed my opportunity. If I had shot Renlo in his head, he would have died instantly and had no chance to ask God for the forgiveness of his sins. If heaven were real, his opportunity to ascend there wouldn't exist, thus sending him to hell by default, I thought to myself.

As I contemplated the missed opportunity to end the war with the West End, Prince stated, "Look, no one wants to see little kids get shot. I'm sure we can all come to some sort of understanding that we are all comfortable with."

Eventually, Renlo spoke, "Prince, since your lackey threatened my life and demanded that my gang own up to a murder we didn't commit, some sort of comeuppance must be rendered for the peace treaty to remain intact. I'm very offended by your consigliere's accusations and threats. You and I both know that I want no harm to come to young kids, especially those named Deuce."

As Renlo mocked me by mentioning Deuce's name, I clutched my pistol tightly and contemplated pulling my pistol a second time. But this time, if I pulled my gun, I planned to live out my dad's advice about only pulling guns to kill. I was going to kill him if I raised my pistol a second time.

Luckily, cooler heads prevailed following the meeting of the minds. Initially, there was no war, but there was no peace, just appeasement to slow down what was inevitable. A clash between two hoods that disliked each other for reasons unbeknownst to one another. Due to Prince's desire to avoid conflict, the opposition was given an extra day to play ball at the blacktop court. In exchange for the extra day, the West End promised to keep their tomfoolery restricted to their side of town. The West End's vile acts consisted of robbing the elderly, conducting reckless drive-by shootings that killed innocent civilians and snitching on other hoods when they got caught. I wish I could say that I was surprised that the crew took such a weak position, but I wasn't. Because everyone remembered the not-so-fun and turbulent times during our youth when it wasn't even safe for grade-schoolers to stand at bus stops. For fear that they would be harmed by assailants that grew tired of waiting for an opportunity to kill their older siblings. When Prince and I left that meeting, he spoke to me in a manner that he hadn't before. He was exasperated and concerned. "H, you messed up, homie. While I understand why you wanted to kill that dummy, you broke one of our core commandments." Even though I didn't realize it during the meeting of the minds, I immediately knew what Prince was referring to. In unison, we both stated, "Never reveal a weakness to an enemy." If an enemy knows what you love or care about, they can attack what means the most to you.

After the contentious meeting of the minds, I remember being so furious at the Nothing to Lose Crew when they decided not to go to war with the West End, I visited my older cousin OG Rock to vent. After the meeting with the Anything to Appease crew, I asked Tee to drive me and my little brother Deuce to my cousin's house. I could always count on Tee's fast and furious driving skills to get me to my desired location in record time. Sensing my frustration, Tasha exceeded the speed limit by at least twelve miles per hour to shorten our commute.

Tee had this innate ability to discern when something was awry when it came to me. During the car ride, she didn't say much. She just bopped her head from side to side as classic tunes blared from her stereo. At one point during the car ride, she turned around and quickly tickled Deuce with one hand as she guided her Nissan's steering wheel with her free hand while asking Deuce what he wanted to listen to. Deuce was young, but he had an old soul. Without hesitation, Deuce started singing about the eyes that didn't know how to smile until the love of his life came into his life, which prompted Tee to immediately queue up "Show and Tell" by Al Wilson, a bonafide classic romantic song. As we neared my cousin's home, we all crooned in unison about the soul that love had taken control of and the desire to feel reciprocated love.

"This is what happens when you raise the babies right. They end up appreciating great music. Classic R&B music that speaks to the soul every Saturday morning. Thank you, Soul Train!" Tee joked as she shifted the car gear to park and stopped in front of the parking space outside of my cousin's modern yet mundane condo. There was something special about waking up early on a peaceful Saturday morning and enjoying breakfast with your family. Watching the Apollo, followed by viewing Soul Train and paying attention to every memorable moment that the legendary artists delivered while Don Cornelius hosted the classic show. I longed for and missed those joyous days.

The joy and distraction of riding while harmonizing along to Al Wilson's song with two of my favorite people quickly gave way to the angst and anger that was polluting my mind due to the earlier meeting with my crew.

After exiting Tee's car and making my way up five grey steps tattered with random splashes of orange, I rapidly knocked until an agitated Rock opened the door. Ignoring me, Rock immediately zeroed in on Deuce, his younger cousin and bizarrely proclaimed, "This mofo 12!"

Tee became highly annoyed and replied, "Kneegrow, what are you talking about? Deuce is nine, and it's abundantly clear from his height that he's nine," as she threw her hands up in exasperation. "How do you not know the age of your own cousin? Rock, are you high?"

"First off, I don't put the poison that is marijuana in my temple, but this mofo right here is without question Twelve," Rock proclaimed again. As I grew increasingly agitated by Rock's antics, I attempted to step from the porch into his home, only to be forcibly denied entry by my cousin as he shook his head in complete and utter disgust. "Look fam, I love you and Deuce to death, but Twelve shall never find sanctuary in my home," he exclaimed as he pointed to Deuce's shirt. After Tee and I glanced at each other with confusion, our eyes made a beeline to examine what Rock was pointing at. It all started to make sense. Deuce was a huge fan of the Ninja Turtles and was rocking a Master Splinter t-shirt. As Tee and I finally arrived at the nonsensical conclusion that in this instance, 1+1 equaled 3, I inhaled deeply and exhaled my frustration as my cousin continued to talk.

My cousin continued, "We can have this conversation on the porch, or my little cousin can absolve himself of his police sins by flipping that shirt with the rat on it, inside out. Once the rat is no longer safely harbored by Deuce, you all may step foot into my humble abode."

"Rock, you might not smoke weed, but you high off something else," Tee proclaimed while shaking her head from side to side. Rock fired back, "Tee, I don't smoke or drink.... I just get high off life. High off life," he reiterated while nodding his head and staring off towards the clouds in the sky.

All of this occurred while I was taking Deuce's shirt off and flipping it inside out to comply with my cousin's asinine request.

Once Deuce's shirt was flipped inside out, and the rat that was Master Splinter was no longer present, a relieved Rock welcomed Deuce by saying, "I love you to death fam, but 12 gives me the heebie-jeebies." A very confused Deuce wandered into our cousin's home. On that day, I secured support from my cousin and the South Side for the imminent war brewing with the West End, but that alliance wasn't easily struck. Family or not, Rock was a businessman and only made moves when it made financial sense to him. "Business, never personal cuzzo," he stated as we greeted each other with a final handshake before Deuce and I headed to Tee's car.

My cousin Rock was a fascinating individual. He had survived many wars in his younger years and was well-respected by all sides of Tree Port. Rock and my other cousin

Tory had always managed to be forward thinkers when it came to maximizing profits while avoiding prison time. While I would have preferred to holler at my cousin Tory about the happenings in Tree Port, I chose not to do so, as he was happily married with a young kid to care for. Our family was important to Tory, and unlike OG Rock, he made moves out of love even if it didn't make financial sense. Nevertheless, I appreciated having two older cousins in my corner who knew how to navigate the streets and corporate America successfully.

Dr. King's non-violent approach was the path my hood chose when the elderly woman was shot, but this time things were different. A nine-year-old boy had passed away due to a foolish dispute at the basketball court. Unlike when the older adult got shot, my hood wasn't on board with giving the West End a pass this time. Some people in our crew said sayonara to the nonviolent approach and made their stances abundantly clear when the crew met up following that 9-year-old little boy's death. No Haitian Revolutionary tales were uttered to encourage my squad to take up arms this time. Several Nothing to Lose members were ready for whatever. Long gone were the days when we deferred to the wishes and guidance of our optimistic de facto leader Prince who had granted the West End an extra day at the basketball court. Silent alliances were formed in various combinations with everyone in the crew except Santino. No one wanted Santino to be involved in the streets. Santino had a promising basketball career that we all respected. Not involving Santino in our street politics was one of the wisest moves my crew ever made as he went on to become what he was destined to be, a shining star that gave so many people hope in Tree Port.

As my dreams recounting my younger years came to a close, I woke up and reflected on the past a bit. Tree Port had managed to win that war but lost something much more important during those turbulent times and conflict-ridden days.

Once I was fully awake, I turned on the television as I attempted to leave days of yesteryear in the past. Much to my chagrin, I woke up to the news of some fool who runs the country, stating that there was violence on both sides in Charlottesville. White supremacists organized a march in Charlottesville and were confronted by counter-protestors. One of the protesters was mowed down by a car driven by a white nationalist, which prompted the person who took over the White House after President Obama to make dog whistle statements that confirmed his support of white supremacists. The 45th President had unequivocally compared white supremacists to those that were protesting white supremacy. The protestors had no history of being adorned in white sheets with hoods, burning crosses, or lynching black people, but the

Clown-in-Chief felt it was appropriate to compare the protesters and white supremacists. In 2017, a sitting President was equating those who would have applauded the murder of Emmett Till to those who were peacefully seeking equality. If there's one thing that America is truly great at, it's refusing to look in the mirror, refusing to acknowledge its negative history and continuously finding new ways to blame the victims of oppression. As I rolled out of my bed and contemplated what to eat for breakfast, I muttered, "F*** Trump."

Today was a big day for the Nothing to Lose crew. Santino was coming into town, and a few of us would be speaking to the youth at the Tree Port Community Center. My hood loved Santino like no other. Throughout his illustrious career, Santino consistently stood up for the disenfranchised and used his platform to give the voiceless a voice, which sometimes cost him endorsements and money. When Eric Garner was deprived of his God-given right to inhale and exhale oxygen, Santino took a stance that offended much of Middle America. I can recall his press conference like it was yesterday. After dropping 23 points and dishing out 9 assists, a reporter dared to ask him why he felt it was appropriate to wear an 'I Can't Breathe' shirt that disparaged policing in America when there was so much black on black violence.

"First off, let me thank you for being foolish enough to ask a question that embodies a racist trope that this country has gotten away with for far too long. Number one, let's set the record straight once and for all. Black on black crime is a myth. I reject this notion that violence in my community should be identified and labeled differently from other intra-community violence in neighborhoods that aren't predominately black. Let me ask you a question. Why don't you care about white-on-white violence, and why don't you and other members of the media classify violence in predominantly white communities as white on white violence? This year, 4,000 murders have been committed by white people against other white people in this country. Ask yourself do you have the same problem or concern about this issue or are those four thousand murders acceptable since white people committed them? Also, crimes in predominately minority areas aren't committed because of one's race; it's based on proximity." The stunned reporter who asked the question was at a loss for words. Santino was smooth like that; he often used his platform to prompt the media and others to think outside of the box.

While Santino had several postgame interviews that stood out, none stood out more than the words he offered when an overzealous cop murdered 12-year-old Tamir Rice for being a brown boy in America. I remember his words so vividly. He walked up to the podium, holding his young son, who was draped in Beautiful Brown Boy Joy attire and proceeded to ignore every question asked by the reporters to share his perspective on police brutality in America.

"Enough is enough. We aren't going to stand for the murders of young black boys and men in our community at the hands of the police. Society can continue to turn a blind eye to the truth while assuming that Black Americans will continue to turn the other cheek. But let's be clear, we have been turning the other cheek for four hundred plus years, and this country still refuses to hold public servants accountable for killing and mistreating Black Americans. This country can continue to try to hide behind the idea that it's just a few bad apples or that it's partially the unarmed black man's fault somehow, but I'm here to tell you that the KKK members that have infiltrated the police force cannot hide under their hoods any longer. I'm lifting the veil. It's not bad training. It isn't our refusal to comply that is driving these acts of brutality. It's pure unadulterated hate. The hate that drove public servants such as judges, attorneys and countless other professionals to hide under sheets while committing atrocities against the Original Man during the 1800s, is still in existence today. The hate from the Jim Crow era lives on and continues to drive the murders of unarmed black men. An officer placing his knee on a subdued man's neck for an extended period of time isn't a failure in training. It's a failure to respect human life. My 3-year-old son knows that he can't choke his pet fish for forty-five seconds and expect it to live. But you want me to buy the idea and nonsense that these officers are good people that need better training so that they don't choke black men who can't breathe to death. We can't breathe, we can't exist, and we can't mind our business in this country without America's racism finding a new way to kill us. We're not going to stand for it anymore. America, you now have a real problem on your hands. Enough individuals have a shared consciousness and understanding of the systemic racism and oppression that this country is guilty of. In the past, this country and the COINTELPRO were able to stop our forward-thinking leaders like Dr. King, Fred Hampton and Malcolm X by killing them. Some people say we need a new leader like Malik el-Shabazz, MLK, Fred Hampton, or Patrice Lumumba. The government already stated decades ago that it would prevent the rise of a Black Messiah. They can and will murder important leaders, but they can't kill shared ideas and principles that are rooted in achieving common goals. When people are united and when thousands are willing to sacrifice their lives, the desire for freedom can't be denied or stopped."

Santino had accomplished some remarkable feats on the court, but his resume was even more impressive off the court. His commitment to our plight and improving the community was unbelievable and inspiring.

As I contemplated Santino's greatness and his

remarkable on and off the court accomplishments, I started to get dressed for the important day that was on the horizon. I made my way to my nifty closet and selected my Properly Stated attire for the day. After quickly getting dressed, I exited my condo, headed to my front door and took off in my Audi. After fifteen minutes of driving and vibing to music, I arrived at my destination, the Tree Port Community Center. It had been years since I last set foot in the community center. As I exited my car and walked towards the entrance, I spotted the chipped bricks on the building that memorialized deuce bullets that were fired at Prince but instead had taken the life of someone else. The Nothing to Lose crew had gone years without having any actual involvement in the streets, but we were still highly respected in Tree Port, which in turn produced an enormous turnout. Santino was scheduled to speak to the rumbustious crowd. Prince would be speaking and so would Tee and I. As I entered the building, I spotted a few of my family members. My mom, my grandma adorned in her colorful church hat and my cousin Tory were all in attendance. I acknowledged my family members by nodding my head and waving as I settled into my seat.

Once I was seated, Santino gave me a fist bump and whispered, "knock 'em out, champ." "You know it," I replied as I continued to scan the auditorium. After carefully scanning the room, Tee and I made eye contact, but there was no greeting exchanged as Tee was extremely upset with me for a myriad of reasons. Santino looked puzzled for a few seconds once he realized that Tee and I didn't greet each other. As I pondered Tee's upcoming wedding and the everlasting impact that it would inevitably have on our friendship, I heard the host say, "Put your hands together for Tree Port's own, undefeated lawyer extraordinaire, Hassan Johnson." It felt magical to hear the words undefeated before my name. But it disturbed me quite a bit as that title would potentially be without merit in a few weeks unless I could figure out a way to beat the charges that my latest client was facing. After taking a few moments to bask in the crowd's thunderous applause and loud screams from Big Momma and my mom, I took my position at the podium. In my opening remarks, I thanked the organizers and citizens of Tree Port for inviting me to speak.

"It's an overwhelming feeling to stand here before you and share a bit about my journey. When I was your age, I wasn't nearly as intelligent and thoughtful as you are. My environment, fears and lack of moral clarity shaped a lot of my foolish decisions. It wasn't until I realized how much my younger brother Deuce looked up to me that I started to make wiser decisions. What's more important than being the best possible example to your siblings and taking care of your family? Nothing, absolutely nothing. Nothing is more important than being an inspiration to those you care most about and being able to look at yourself in the mirror every day and be proud of the reflection you see. Beyond prioritizing our families, we also have the potential to have an enormous impact on our community. With so many negative factors working in concert to suppress your true potential, we have to acknowledge and accept that all we have in this world is each other. Systemic oppression is real. Oppression is daunting, unrelenting and strives to defeat us in every facet of our life. How can we negate oppression to the best of our abilities?

"First, we must recognize that our most potent counterpunch lies within educating ourselves economically. A President once said, 'It's the economy stupid.' The economy has never been set up to work in our favor. When I realized that I wanted to attend law school, it was the brotherly and sisterly love of Tree Port that made it possible. My closest friends came together and decided that I would get to law school by any means possible. After completing law school, my attention shifted to doing something for my family that had never been done. My wonderful grandma and mom, who are in attendance today, never owned a house before we embarked on the save 3.5% challenge. If you have never heard of the 3.5 percent challenge, let me take a few moments to explain the key components. It's a challenge and promise to save 3.5 percent for a down payment and give it to someone you consider family once all three of their credit scores are above 680 for a down payment on a house. Saving 3.5% required sacrifices that I was initially uneasy about. I was accustomed to taking lengthy vacations, taking my girlfriend to Capital Grille frequently and using Uber all the time. With this challenge, I had to shorten the length of my vacations, use Uber less and cut back on enjoying delectable meals at fancy restaurants. After graduating from law school, I told my mom and grandma if they used the next year and a half to fix their credit, I would ensure that they had the 3.5% down payment to purchase their first home. One of the first things we did after embarking on the 3.5% challenge was to analyze their credit reports.

"We pulled their annual credit reports and created a sound strategy to resolve any outstanding debts that could negatively impact their dream of purchasing a home. Next, we identified and focused on the loans and credit cards with the highest interest rate and paid those items off first. Those are just some of the steps we took to break the predatory lending cycle that cost so many of us thousands of extra dollars in interest during our lifetime. After their credit scores from all three credit bureaus crossed the 680 score threshold, we were deliberate in our next steps. We sought out a black realtor and hired a black law firm for the closing process. We must support and patronize black businesses as frequently as possible. When black economics are discussed, we often focus on the negative. Some individuals believe the ills in our community exist because we don't support black businesses enough.

"I vehemently disagree with this notion. We do support each other. Think about it. Many of us frequent black barbershops and hair salons monthly. A lot of us tithe weekly at black churches. Tithing alone is ten percent and a display of tremendous support. That's the same percentage that some of us pay in taxes. Let's start imploring our churches to build more businesses and pathways for us to buy black. Just because churches have non-exempt tax status shouldn't mean that we constantly give freely and gleefully and expect no return on our investment. Shout out to the real and caring pastors in Tree Port that do give back to the community. We appreciate you, and we need more leaders like you.

"Back to one of my initial points, whenever you feel yourself spending too frivolously, tell yourself, 'it's the economy stupid,' as a means to refocus on saving and buying black when possible. I've challenged myself to make sure I support as many black businesses as I can. When buying gifts for family members or friends, my first stop is the Official Black Wall Street App and WeBuyBlack.com. To truly be free, we need to be debt-free and empowered economically. Let's continue to think outside of the box while leveraging our culture to elevate our communities as a whole. If one of us is drowning, we all are drowning.

"Before I take my seat, I would like to address a topic that's frequently tossed about nationally and wrongly addressed in the Tree Port Tribune newspaper. Black on black violence. This notion that black people are their own worst enemies emerged from racists and is often parroted by some in our community. It's a notion frequently espoused by those who feel they have achieved some modicum of success that gives them the right to critique others without ever taking their circumstances into fair consideration. When you analyze it closely, the black middle class and bourgeois tier have in many ways inadvertently become a proxy for white supremacy ideology unbeknownst to them. I like President Obama, and I believe he means well, but anytime your assessments of Black Americans' ills are rooted in negative black pathology, you're most likely wrong. Black people aren't in the predicament that we are in today because we don't value education enough, or ill-advised spending habits or because we don't work hard enough. We are primarily in our current predicament because systematic racism is ever-evolving and has this innate ability to metastasize into new forms of oppression. It doesn't matter how hard we work or how educated we become. Systemic oppression spreads rapidly and is highly contagious. For every new door that we knock down or pry open, racism attempts to close three.

"People are highly and rightfully upset at Kanye West for his statement that slavery was a choice, but don't direct the same energy at President Obama's stance of opposing reparations during his presidency. Which voice and perspective carry more weight with the world and in our community? The out-of-touch words of a genius producer or the first Black President giving systemic oppression a pass by not supporting reparations?

"We often attack celebrities we don't like and give those that we admire a pass even when we know they're wrong. We have deified some individuals based on their accomplishments and positioned them as being beyond valid critique. No one is above reproach or legitimate critique. I can't stand up here and pretend I have a solution to a problem that has reigned supreme for over 400 years in this country. But, I can tell you that paths to ownership and prioritizing our community first might be our best option to inoculate ourselves as much as possible against the vile virus that is systemic oppression. Prioritizing our neighborhoods doesn't mean we mistreat others. It just means we acknowledge that our family, friends and communities matter the most to us.

"Oh yeah, one last thought before I take my seat, I want to speak about something that even I have been guilty of doing at times. When we engage in black pathology, we often unfairly critique Black Americans while uplifting other model minority groups that we feel our community should emulate. This idea that others magically show up in America with nothing and become middle class or upper-middle-class in mass numbers is a lie. Be analytical for just a few minutes and refrain from using antidotal examples of other groups going from nothing to something. In fact, how can a person with absolutely nothing make it from their homeland and travel to the United States across the Pacific or Atlantic Oceans with absolutely no money or support?

"Maybe I'm unaware of this new ability that people have to swim or walk across water as if they're the Son of God without a dollar to their names.

"Has any immigrant group accomplished more than, let's say, the top performing 5% of African Americans? I don't think so. The path to the middle class in America is hard. A few things that may help us reach the middle class are homeownership, buying more robust life insurance policies and supporting ourselves as much as possible. If we purchase from black businesses 8% of the time, let's double that number to 16% in the next year here in Tree Port. Let's grow together. Let's be great together! Thank you to the Tree Port Community Center staff for inviting me to speak and allowing me to share a little about myself. Tree Port, thank you for listening to my unfiltered thoughts on a myriad of topics. Tree Port, I love you!" I stated in closing as I left the podium and bid the audience adieu. As I strolled back to my seat, the only thing that I could think about was my younger brother Deuce. My day would have been made if Deuce would have been in attendance and able to hear the speech that I spent many nights toiling over.

If the audience was applauding as I made my exit from the podium, I didn't hear it. I was mesmerized by the young faces in the crowd who seemed to have enjoyed my words. My words must have resonated with my friends as well because Tee acknowledged me by cracking half a smile as I settled into my seat.

As I found remnants of joy in Tee's smile, I heard the host of the event state, "Next up to the podium is Tree Port's own Santino Brown." I anticipated some of the pro-black sentiment that was sprinkled in Santino's speech, but I had no idea that he would be so unapologetic in his condemnation of America's treatment of black people. In the wake of the recent Las Vegas massacre, I expected Santino's handlers to alter some of the content in his speech as any subsequent blowback from his message could jeopardize his endorsement deals. Yet, there he was, standing at the podium draped in an ultra-black Colin Kaepernick jersey and a green and yellow hat with a black power fist emerging through the color red. The look of determination in his eyes reminded me of a simmering hurricane. It reminded me of a dangerous storm, circling in the middle of the ocean to accumulate the necessary fury to evolve into a category five machine of destruction. The determination and defiance of Nat Turner were alive and well in the wrath of Santino's piercing eyes.

"It's truly a blessing to be amongst the youth of Tree Port that I care so deeply for. It's a privilege and honor to be part of a panel that includes my distinguished lifelong friend Tasha, or as many in Tree Port affectionately call her, Tee. And I can't forget about my great friends Hassan and Prince. During our young years, we had no idea what life had in store for us. No one could have imagined that Hassan would graduate from law school with no student loan debt and go on to become an outstanding lawyer who has won eleven cases and suffered no defeats. Eleven victories and not one L in the courtroom! That's incredible. That's inspiring! One day he might surpass the 15-0 winning streak that I established at Tree Port's legendary blacktop court. Who knows?

"No one knew or envisioned that Tee would become the incredible woman that she is today. Not a single person in our neighborhood could foresee Tasha maturing into a well-respected community advocate fighting for fair and equal policing in an area that has historically struggled to find common ground with law enforcement. And who knew that dribbling and shooting a basketball would create so many endless opportunities for my family and me. While some of us are successfully living out our dreams, we must never forget that our dreams exist within the context of a 400-year nightmare that America refuses to wake up from. It's a manufactured dream or opportunity that genuinely only exists for a small percentage of our people.

"Miraculously, our aspirations and talents have managed to flourish despite systemic oppression. To be black and achieve a portion of the American dream speaks to our community's resilience passed down by individuals like Fannie Lou Hamer, Harriet Tubman and countless others who sacrificed their lives to create a palatable passageway for us. The trail to freedom that they fought so hard to bring to fruition lives as a mirage in a waterless desert that's masquerading as the American Dream. It's a nightmare that says now is not the appropriate time to protest inequality and injustice. It's the loud voice of ignorance that attempts to misconstrue peaceful protests such as kneeling during the National Anthem as disrespect towards the flag and members of the military.

"Am I in the same country that shed crocodile tears when the great Muhammad Ali passed away? Before his death, America only lauded and praised the boisterous Muhammad Ali as a national hero when he could no longer vocally express his dissent and ire at the mistreatment of Black people by this nation. When the great Dr. Martin Luther King was alive, he was classified as an agitator and uppity Negro who didn't know how to stay in his place, even though the protests he led promoted unity and peace. Is this the same country that didn't even play the National Anthem before 2009 but decided to start doing so after receiving millions of dollars from the same military that it proclaims to love oh so dearly?

"I tell my young son consistently; I just reside and pay taxes in the United States. My loyalty is not to a flag or country. My loyalty is to my family, my friends and the Tree Port community. Consistently, I see the national media stating that our community is nothing more than a cesspool of ignorance littered with black on black crime. First off, what is black on black crime? It's a racist trope rooted in Jim Crow ideology that proclaims that Black Americans are inherently more violent than others. Black on black crime is consistently and conveniently trotted out as a counterattack by the media and politicians whenever we demand America be true to its promise of equality and freedom. If Black Americans were inherently violent, I'm sure our response to slavery, Jim Crow and unjustified police shootings would look a lot different from the peaceful protests we have utilized to combat our unfair treatment. When it comes to violence, one must look beyond the headlines. Violence is based on proximity and is often rooted in retaliation. Retaliation is a core component in how the military responds to acts deemed aggressive and hostile. How then is the violence in Tree Port different from the acts of war committed by Presidents of the United States when missile strikes are authorized, knowing that hundreds of children will die just to kill one or two terrorists? Do we view community violence differently than civilian casualties of war because geopolitical conflicts are coordinated and authorized by well-dressed men and women in Washington whom society has deemed intelligent? What's more admirable, a person who presides over a country that's protected by two oceans killing individuals overseas for hidden capitalistic reasons under the guise of anti-terrorism? Or a young person in Tree Port exacting revenge on someone who killed a member of their family?

"I say none of this to absolve those that kill in Tree Port. I'm sharing this comparison to encourage the youth to be better than the people in power in Washington, D.C. Be better than the Nothing to Lose crew that I grew up with. Before you dim the lights of an individual and send their soul spiraling to hell, think about the ramifications of what comes with that decision. It doesn't bring your family member back, and it continues a never-ending vicious cycle of violence that the young people in Tree Port are forced to navigate. The ill-advised decisions you make today may become the reason you never fulfill your true potential. With your knowledge, intellect and desire to win, you have it in you to be greater than 11-0.

Be something greater than a basketball player who has aspirations of making it to the NBA. Learn to nourish and cultivate the unique spirit that resides deep inside you. Know thou greatness. Don't settle for being the G-O-A-T. Become the best possible version of yourself. Be the Knewgoat!" yelled Santino as he brought his rousing speech to a close.

Santino's words of wisdom and the astuteness he showcased while explaining life in Tree Port weren't surprising. During our youth, Santino loved two things dearly, playing basketball and reading books. When he wasn't playing ball, he was reading; when he wasn't reading, he was playing ball. Reading and learning history from the OGs was how our crew acquired most of our knowledge. Santino was well versed in America's original sins. His success and money didn't distort his perspective of what being a Black man in America meant. He still saw and understood the challenges and obstacles that we encounter every day.

At a very young age, we became accustomed to being accosted by cops and being accused of crimes that even the worst of us in Tree Port weren't capable of committing at the adolescent ages of eleven and twelve. White and black cops had a knack for criminalizing the young boys in Tree Port as soon as we stepped foot outside of the confines of our public housing apartments. My first interaction with the Tree Port Police Department left a lasting impression that made me despise and distrust cops. At the young and tender age of ten years old, a police cruiser erratically sped up to the basketball court with little regard for my safety while I was making my way to the entrance of Tree Port's legendary blacktop court. As I was attempting to open the silver gate to enter the court, two police officers hastily emerged from their patrol car with their guns drawn and yelled, "Put your god d*** hands in the air! And drop everything in your hands right now!" Remembering what my mom taught me from the day I exited her womb, I immediately obeyed the officers' commands, which caused me to drop my brand new mechanical pencil. My newly purchased mechanical pencil shattered into pieces as the officers pointed guns at me that paralyzed my body with an indescribable fear. I had longed and begged for that purple and black mechanical pencil for a while and was looking forward to using it for the first time at school the following day. The pencil that I intended to toss up in the air before taking notes during class was instead resting in bits and pieces on the ground near my tennis shoes. I would rather lose my dream pencil than risk being shot and killed by overzealous police officers. After I dropped my pencil, one of the cops forcibly slammed me into the basketball court entrance gate. The impact of hitting the gate was so hard that the lines from the gate were still distinctly imprinted on my face when I returned home hours later and glanced at my reflection in the mirror. I wish I could say that my interaction with the cops was a rare occurrence for the youth in Tree Port, but it wasn't. Every single person in my crew experienced cops harassing them for no reason at all. At some point, I suppose we became numb to how the cops treated us and just found ways to cope with it while hoping and praying that our mothers would never be on television talking about how White Jesus told them to forgive the cops that killed one of us. As I reflected on days gone by from my younger years, Santino left the podium and headed towards his seat.

A proud and elated Tee jumped to her feet and interrupted Tino's short strides with an exuberant hug and words of encouragement. "Superstar on the court, but even more important off the court," she stated while smiling and clutching Tino tightly. My eyes once again shifted to the dazzling rock on Tee's ring finger while her hands rested on Tino's back as they embraced. That diamond signified that I would be losing my friend and imaginary potential wife. As the dazzling gem that had been forged by the earth and volcanic lava continued to glitter, I relived my last cordial conversation with Tee.

6

7/5 BORN TO LEAD 12

A few weeks before the Tree Port Community Center event, Tee excitedly called me and screamed to the heavens, "Hassan! I have great news that I must share in person." Hastily, I ended the call and began to prepare for one of our epic celebrations that had become somewhat routine over the years. Whenever Tee or I accomplished a remarkable career feat, we celebrated by enjoying Uncle Nearest Whiskey on the rocks first, a glass of Chianti second and Godiva chocolate as that was Tee's favorite. While shuffling around the house, I grabbed my favorite whiskey and pristine crystal glasses for our drinks. I collected a few pieces of chocolate as my excitement for what I presumed to be a promotion for Tee reached its peak. Any promotion that Tee earned was well deserved. She had spent countless hours doing the dirty work required to better the community, while many others only showed up for photo ops that promoted their organizations. She truly loved and understood the youth in Tree Port and had found a way to forge genuine bonds with the youngsters that were even foreign to Prince and me. She had this smooth and uncanny penchant for disarming the most cynical people in society. She could sell a cracked seashell to an already protected clam or a hump to a camel that had no room for an additional hump. She was simply one of the most amazing women in the world.

As my preparation for her arrival neared its end, I heard a knock. It was a gentler knock from Tee than I was accustomed to. One hundred percent of the time, she delivered that annoying hard police knock to troll my calm sensibilities. Every time she arrived, she would knock hard, and before opening the door, I would yell, "who that? Twelve?" She would reply, "boy, you know this ain't no cop, open the door."

As I opened the door while wondering why she didn't knock like Twelve for the first time, I noticed it. Tee had knocked gingerly on the door as a means to protect the flawless diamond that meant forever with someone had been determined. My heart and mind started racing immediately. Which hand is the ring finger on...? Is it the right, or is it the left? I anxiously pondered.

As my reflections of days gone by came to a close, professionally dressed Tasha made her way to the podium. While Tee was well versed on the topics that Tino and I covered, her message focused on a different subject. Her topic was often ignored when discussing crime. She zeroed in on how to best protect black women and what role black men in the community should play to protect our women. With such ease, she spliced and explained the reported homicides, rapes and domestic violence numbers. Tee initiated her speech by stating, "Tree Port, good evening. Today I would like to delve into a topic that's near and dear to my heart. How do we protect black women? Lost in the common headlines of the Tree Port Tribune are the stories of so many women who suffer violence at the hands of their partners or strangers. I'm imploring and challenging the young boys and young men in Tree Port to reverse these trends and stand up for what's right and protect the Queens of the community. As it pertains to women, respect shouldn't just be reserved for your mom, grandma, sisters, or cousins. Respect should be your default disposition when interacting with young ladies. When women in our community are in vulnerable positions, extra care and protection should be extended to them. Show us that you love us as we love you. We love each one of you dearly. We march and we cry out whenever harm unjustly comes your way. We stand on the front line, front and center, every time you need us. We make sacrifices daily not out of obligation but out of self-love first and foremost, and because our desire to become the best versions of ourselves can no longer be brushed aside as an afterthought. We pursue our aspirations and become entrepreneurs in record numbers because our dreams will no longer be deferred or obstructed by outdated ways of thinking.

"Your safety is one of the core reasons we have worked so diligently to acquire bachelor's degrees at the highest rate in America, but it isn't the only reason. Our well-being and safety matter just as much as yours. Black women go above and beyond the call of duty to provide a safe and nourishing environment for black boys. In return, we are requesting that the love you have for us becomes more apparent in how you treat, respect and protect us. Young brothers out there, protect your community at all costs. Don't treat your hustle, your friends or your quest for success with more dignity and respect than you treat the ladies who have made protecting you their number one priority. Protect us the same way we protect you. We love you and we know that you love us too."

Tasha made her way back to her seat after giving a memorable speech as she had done on so many occasions before. Tino immediately stood up and hugged Tee before lauding the amazing speech she had just shared with Tree Port's youth. "Tee, that was incredible. Why do you always have to one-up me? I would be in real trouble if you played ball," Santino joked as they embraced. I greeted Tee with no words but cracked a smile that exuded how proud I was of her. Even when we weren't on the same page, our respect and admiration for one another always remained intact.

Anytime she needed me, I was always there, and anytime I needed her, she was there. On so many occasions, before I could even call to ask for help, Tee managed to be present. From the outside looking in, I completely understood why my crew and her friends always clamored for us to explore our bond beyond just being friends. I understood why our respective inner circles felt Tee and I falling for one another was inevitable and destined to be.

As it pertains to dating, I had been fortunate. I consistently met and dated top-notch sisters. The wider circumference surrounding Tree Port had no shortage of educated and cute black women. The three times that I ended up in long-term relationships, I was the one who walked away, even though all three relationships would have led to marriage for ninety-nine percent of men. I was an enigma of sorts when it came to long-term commitment. I enjoyed gallivanting around the world, trying new wines with a dime and two-stepping to music in foreign countries as singers uttered beautiful words I didn't understand.

Nevertheless, around the year and a half mark when the women in my life would start meandering on the idea of engagement or marriage, I would become uneasy and begin to hatch an escape plan. Not because I feared marriage and not because I feared being with one woman for a lifetime. I could never quite put my finger on the exact root cause of what prompted me to run from long-term commitments. I just knew that I wanted something more than the traditional marriage where your income doubles.

I needed something more than the cookie-cutter family where you have two kids and post lovely photos on Instagram in matching outfits for holiday pictures. What's the purpose of projecting an amazing relationship for social media when in reality, your marriage is treading in a puddle of mediocrity and disappointment? That's not what love is supposed to be. By in large, I viewed marriage as a societal norm that was forced on people. I had seen matrimony lead many down a path of pain. My life had been miserable enough. I had no interest in potentially condemning myself to a 40-year sentence of misery. I longed not for a lady I could take on nice dates or one that carefully curated her social media presence as a medium to show off our relationship. My most intimate moments were not up for sale for likes or some sort of trophy of happiness that disappeared like a false mirage when examined closely. I wanted something more. I wanted to be understood. I desired a loyal woman that I could be my authentic self around. I desired a real love and unbreakable commitment that most people couldn't fathom or imagine.

Once upon a time, I walked away from a sweet and intelligent lawyer, an incredible social worker with a giving heart, and lastly, a dentist that had a smile that lit up the world. I was accustomed to walking away from quality women with little to no hesitation, but on the night that Tee excitedly announced her engagement, walking away pierced my soul. As soon as she uttered the words, "I'm getting married," she immediately noticed the blank expression on my face and saw fraught intertwined with disappointment in my eyes. That night wasn't the first time that Tee and I had a tough conversation about our friendship. One night as we were walking home from a party during our collegiate years, Tee reached over and caressed my hand. As our palms started to sweat in excitement from the potential of what could be, she decided to finally relinquish her innermost feelings when she expressed that she believed with all of her heart that we could be something special. In response to Tee sharing how she felt about me, I was dead silent. Can you imagine that? An individual with a robust lexicon who would become a lawyer later in life was speechless around his best friend. Tasha was accustomed to me freely sharing my deepest thoughts and feelings about everything, but on that night, I only shared fear. Tee was exceptional at selling bad ideas so imagine how impressive she was at marketing good ones. And this was a great idea. It was the same idea that the Nothing to Lose crew had always been fond of and determined to see come to fruition one day. It was the same idea that Santino, Prince and even Deuce seemed to think was brilliant. Before Tee and I ever imagined it or held hands romantically for the very first time, those closest to us were rooting for our magical moment to happen.

In many ways, we were a perfect match, a match made in heaven like Jimi Hendrix and his guitar. An ideal pairing like Peter Tosh's vocals and the Black experience. Like Magic Johnson and a no-look pass. Even though everyone in our circle assumed we would eventually end up together, we failed to become the perfect match that was Jimi Hendrix and his guitar. Instead, Tee and I were more akin to Icarus and the sun, apart but too close for comfort.

After Tee expressed her thoughts on what we could grow to be, I continued to hold her hand as we remained silent for the last several minutes of our walk. My heart wanted to take the chance and tell her that I agreed and that I felt the same way she did. Yet, I never mustered up the courage to meet her halfway. Instead of telling Tee that I agreed with her assessment that we could be something incredible, I released her hand and said, "Tee, have a good night," when we reached our respective dorm rooms. On that night, I was too scared to turn around and look at her one final time as she walked away. If I had looked at her one more time, I would have been too intrigued and mesmerized to let the love that many felt was destined to be fade into the darkness of fear and regret.

As my daydreaming intensified and my thoughts of rewriting history with Tasha became more lucid, James Brown's legendary record, "Say It Loud – I'm Black and I'm Proud," interrupted my thoughts. As the crowd at the Tree Port Community Center started to rise from their seats in excitement, James Brown sang words about not quitting until we get our share. As Michael Jackson's musical idol implored the crowd to proudly embrace their blackness, the crowd's segment that understood and appreciated timeless music started dancing and shoulder rolling as James Brown made his phenomenal proclamation of being Black and Proud. Not to be outdone by the Black Queens in the crowd who had the remarkable agility to dance to the beat while holding newborns, Prince made a one-of-a-kind entrance. Prince came out shuffling his feet and sliding across the stage floor with the presence of a young Michael Jackson doing the Moonwalk for the first time at "Motown 25: Yesterday, Today and Forever." Prince truly embodied the showmanship of Al Sharpton and Don King, minus the pretentiousness. Even when he planned things, he had the uncanny ability to create memorable moments that seemed organic and spontaneous. After dancing for a minute or so, Prince gave the makeshift DJ the cut the music signal by swiping his hand rapidly past his neck twice. After the crowd calmed down and regained their composure, Prince held up the Black Power fist and said,

"Say It Loud, I'm Black and I'm Proud," while extending the mic for a call and response that allowed the crowd to say it as well. In another lifetime, I swear Prince would have been an incredible mega-church pastor that could convince people to give 20% instead of 10% to his church. As the music faded and the crowd settled in, Prince started his speech.

"First off, I want to say nothing unifies black people like Grandma's cooking or a great record that touches our souls. For a significant portion of my life, I thought I lived and exemplified, 'I'm Black and I'm Proud.' Little did I know I wasn't even close to embodying what it really means to be black and proud. Being black and proud means loving every scintilla of what it means to be black. It also means not being embarrassed to be yourself and embracing our history while understanding that we aren't a monolith. We are a diverse tribe of people who were divorced from our homeland, separated from our original culture and given beliefs that whitewashed our originality. Despite all the challenges and obstacles we have been through, we managed to develop a unique culture that the rest of the world emulates and gravitates to for entertainment and profit. Corporations love to exploit our culture for financial gain, but those same entities hate when we fight for ownership and use our innate talents in a manner that uplifts our people. Whatever skills or attributes God blessed you with, consider using them for the greater good.

Don't buy into the trap that negativity will take you further than positivity.

"On a different note, I would like to discuss two civil rights activists that I admire. During my younger years, Hassan and I would pride ourselves on being more like Malcolm X than Martin Luther King. I had the audacity and unmitigated gall to diminish the great Martin Luther King by implying that he was soft or unwilling to confront systemic oppression and racism in the way that was needed. My stupidity led me to believe that it was fair to criticize the man who led marches, was arrested countless times and ultimately lost his life due to his commitment and devotion to achieving equality. Dr. Martin Luther King's sacrifice and approach must never be disrespected and diminished by those, including myself that benefit from the path he blazed. MLK, Fannie Lou Hamer, John Lewis, Malcolm X, Stokely Carmichael, Shirley Chisholm and countless others devoted their lives to the pursuit of equality to help us inch closer to the mountaintop that MLK dreamt of but never lived to see. Dr. King was able to imagine what is unseen in the same way that Stevie Wonder's vision can somehow visualize music.

"Dr. King envisioned what is only visible to a dreamer, the pinnacle of freedom that many are too blind to see. Our generation has some nerve in how we perceive this journey towards equality. Many of us reach the middle class and become Black Klansmen or out-of-touch conservatives. We start to believe the pervasive notion that we know what's best for all black people once we achieve a modicum of success. If success compels me to demean my community instead of inspiring it, I don't want it. How can a person know what's best for black people when they haven't devoted the requisite time to studying the intricacies of systemic oppression? Should I feel qualified to speak on Black economics if I don't understand the nuances of how the American economy is set up to make the rich wealthier and to keep the poor downtrodden? The economy is centered on siphoning money from the common woman and man via taxes and disbursing it back to the wealthy via private financial allocation agreements and government contracts. Are such practices not handouts? Why do people that complain anytime the lower class receives benefits remain silent when the wealthy receive benefits? The way we analyze complex problems and reach simple solutions without giving credence to nuance often impacts how we applaud or criticize heroes.

"When I would praise Malcolm's approach to demean Dr. King's direction, it was real idiocy and lunacy mixed with self-aggrandizement. Both men envisioned the same destination for us. They just had different perspectives on the best path to freedom for our people. Malcolm's approach seemed more defiant and rebellious, which made it appealing to me. While I don't think he was wrong at all, my admiration for Malcolm X made me overlook the brilliance of Dr. King's approach. I ignored the strength that it took to embody a non-violent approach in a society that delivered centuries of state-sanctioned violence against us. Dr. King was brilliant and brave. He knew that taking on the racism and hatred embedded in this nation's fabric in an overly confrontational manner would lead to more violence. Incidents like the one captured in the iconic photo of Malcolm X holding the newspaper with the headline, "Seven Unarmed Negroes Shot in Cold Blood by Los Angeles Police," would have become more common. Dr. King understood the power of shame. He leveraged the imagery of sisters and brothers being brutally beaten by cops, attacked by dogs and water sprouting from the hoses held by racists to organize structured protests. Dr. King's strategy led to international media coverage, which produced fundamental societal changes that we still benefit from today. How stupid was I to utter and promote this notion that Dr. King and others should have taken on this unjust system in an overly aggressive and confrontational manner in the 1950s and 1960s? Our world today is still littered with the killings of Trayvon Martin, Tamir Rice and Philando Castile. Imagine how many more of us would have died if my strategy led the march towards freedom.

"I was demanding something from others that I don't

even demand from myself. How many of us are even willing to confront racism head-on when we encounter it at our jobs? We are so frightened and threatened by our fear of racism that we don't always stand up for ourselves when we experience it. Instead of combating racism, we often allow the fear of being without a job and the potential of losing our means to provide for our families to negate what is right and just. We essentially come up with any justification under the sun to explain away our refusal to stand up for what's right. When we experience racism on the job, we fear that the racist individual has the upper hand and that our careers will be in jeopardy if we speak up, even though we should be protected from a Human Resource perspective. How many of us confront or cut off our white friends or co-workers who express anti-black views? Yet, we look at historic and iconic figures that created these paths to success like they didn't do enough. That's the thing about looking in the mirror. We often look at it to adore our own perceived greatness while diminishing the greatness of others. I looked in the mirror and admired myself for going to a few marches, making a few Facebook posts about injustices and supporting black businesses here and there. I was unfairly critiquing one of the most outstanding individuals in our history who laid down his life in a way that I wasn't evaluating myself. I challenged myself to stop critiquing greatness until I accomplish something great. Being named Prince gave me no right or authority to criticize a King.

"How is it that I have all the advice in the world for others but none for my own personal self-improvement? How is it that I extrapolate poorly constructed ideas and clichés and promote them as being the solution for my community when I haven't even successfully elevated my family members and friends with these so-called brilliant ideas of mine? When I first started exclaiming, I'm Black and I'm Proud. Black Excellence this and Black Excellence that. I didn't understand how much white supremacy had impacted my thought process and how I had been pre-programmed to center whiteness as the standard of achievement. Have you ever paid attention to these studies that say black people are trailing whites at this and that? You don't say, is my response to these absurd no context having studies. Why would anyone be surprised that black people are trailing the group that had a four-hundred-year head start? I'm surprised by the progress we have made because the group we are trailing still benefits from judicial and political systems that prevent black people from succeeding en masse.

"To be black and proud is to treat every person with the same empathy and respect that Jesus consistently treated people with. Jesus serves as an exemplary archetype of what it means to be black and proud. He treated a leper, a prostitute and 12 homeless disciples that didn't know how to fish or walk on water like him with the same respect and empathy.

"As we move closer to the mountaintop that MLK spoke of, what does our respect and empathy for one another look like? As we achieve economic success, do we develop an attitude that looks down on those with different economic statuses, vocabularies, dress preferences, or differences that make us slightly uncomfortable? Why are we so quick to attack the victims of systemic oppression instead of the actual system oppressing us? For me, I realized that it's easy to attack the victim because there aren't any repercussions for attacking those that have no retribution power. If you attack the actual system, you may lose your career, à la Colin Kaepernick, or your life, à la Malcolm X. I had to look in the mirror of self-reflection and ask myself, am I willing to address my cowardice and my penchant for making poorly constructed assessments of what ails the community? Why am I constantly absorbing and regurgitating negative ideas about the community without even researching them or pressure testing them for truthfulness? Perhaps we are inclined to believe the worst about our community because it makes us feel better when we accomplish something positive. Whenever we achieve something great, it's a testament to the resolve and strength of those that came before us. Never forget that.

"Santino said it best. The journey to greatness that we are on starts within. Know thou greatness! Don't settle for being the Goat, be something more. Be the Knewgoat!" Prince exclaimed as he closed out his speech and headed back towards the crew.

As Prince made his way back to his seat, I took a final glance at the glimmering rock on Tasha's ring finger and reflected on the engagement announcement that rocked my world.

7

FEAR NO DEATH, FEAR NO HELL

After the debacle that was Tasha's big engagement announcement, I immediately requested an emergency meeting with the good doctor. Dr. Williams was happy to oblige. "At a loss for words, are we Hassan?" Dr. Williams inquired just minutes into our session. I think the doctor was surprised that I wasn't very talkative at the start of our meeting, since I was the one who suddenly requested a session during a week that we weren't scheduled to convene. Just as I had done on several occasions before, I poured myself a glass of wine first and then passed Dr. Williams the McBride Sisters Black Girl Magic bottle and watched her pour herself a glass of wine that I knew she wouldn't taste. During our first few sessions watching Dr. Williams pour my expensive wine into a glass and letting it sit irked me; until I realized that her actions were of little to no consequence. No harm, no foul, as we used to say while shooting hoops at the basketball court during my adolescent days. Eventually, it dawned on me that her untouched glass of wine was just a second glass of wine that I could enjoy when our sessions concluded. As Dr. Williams gently nudged the thin-framed glasses resting on her nose and contemplated asking me if I was still at a loss for words, my scattered thoughts settled, and I asked her, "Dr. Williams, why do you always pour yourself a glass of wine and refuse to drink it? I don't get it. You appear to have great taste based on your attire and accessory selections. Taste that I'm assuming extends to an appreciation for fine wine. Why do you pour fine wine during our sessions just to let it sit? Just to let it go to waste and age as if it's still protected by a barrel?"

Before getting into her real response, she jokingly responded, "Hassan, does the wine that I pour go to waste? Or is it merely a second glass of vino for you once I make my exit?" Before I could offer a retort, Dr. Williams lowered the glass of wine in her hand without drinking from it and continued:

"Hassan, I knew we would reach this day at some point. You want to know how and why I can pour myself a glass of wine and be perfectly content with admiring it versus drinking it: Hassan, one word, discipline. I love drinking wine during my personal time in the confines of my home, and this is an exceptional vino that I would love nothing more than to indulge. However, discipline and the willpower to avoid temptation are essential to keeping a clear mind. Is your mind currently clear?"

"Dr. Williams, I don't know what my mind is doing. It's not clear, but it's not rainstorm cloudy either; perhaps my mind is partially cloudy. One of my closest friends, Tasha, I mean Tee recently got engaged. And while I want to be happy for her, I'm confused about how I really feel. I'm having trouble processing and admitting my true feelings. It's like I only want to see her happy, and she seems happy, but I'm not one-hundred percent happy for her. Does that make sense? It's like I'm losing something special that I could have had but never had."

"Hassan, you don't strike me as a person that lacks the confidence to go after what your heart desires. It sounds like you know what you want, but you're afraid to admit it to yourself for some reason. I'm going to be very candid and deliberate with my next question for you. What's stopping you from pursuing your heart's desire? What's preventing you from asking Tasha to reconsider her engagement?" the doctor inquired.

Before responding to Dr. Williams' question, I reflected on the night when Tasha announced her engagement to me in person. The night that I saw her sparkling diamond for the first time. The evening I learned that she planned to spend her forever with someone else.

On the night that Tasha came by to tell me she was engaged, she immediately hugged me and did her happy dance as she flaunted her stunning ring by waving it side to side, inches away from my face. "Wow. Wow, Tee. I can't believe it; the apple of every man's eye in Tree Port is officially off the market." I was in complete and sheer shock that Tee was going to marry someone else. As I struggled to regain my composure, I managed to utter a half-hearted congrats. Sensing the fakeness in my congratulations, Tasha's happiness and excitement quickly diminished.

"Hassan, I show up to tell you the biggest news of my life, and your response is a half-hearted congrats? What's really good?"

As I struggled to find the appropriate words to respond with, Tasha made her way to the Uncle Nearest Whiskey and grabbed the glass I had set on the table before she arrived. She poured herself a drink but added no rocks of ice to comfort her room temperature libation. After pouring a few whiskey shots into the empty glass, she sunk into the right side of the couch and sipped her warm spirit. To create some much-needed distance between us, I opted to sit on the couch's opposite end, the far left side.

"Tee, do you love Darren deeply? Are you getting married for the right reasons, or are you just settling?" I inquired.

Frustrated with my line of questioning, Tee took a few deep breaths and uttered, "Hassan, I can't believe you. On what's supposed to be the best day of my life, my best friend of twenty plus years is trying to ruin my night," she stated as she started to become visibly upset. "Of course, I love the man that I'm planning to marry."

After processing her proclamation of love for Darren, I attempted to quell the tension. "I guess this means that Santino was wrong. I won't be marrying an AKA," I joked as I tried to lift her spirits and improve the mood. The fellas had this ongoing wager that I would undoubtedly end up marrying an AKA or Delta as I frequently ended up dating women that belonged to one of those organizations somehow.

"Tee, if you're truly happy, I'm happy for you," I stated while staring off into space to avoid making eye contact with her. Sensing that our conversation would fail to evolve to a place of genuine congratulations and happiness, Tee quickly downed her whiskey and rose from the right end of the couch and made her way towards the door.

While fiddling with the bronze door handle, Tee turned around and stated, "Hassan, you do know that I couldn't wait forever to see if your heart would ever heal to a place where you are capable of giving me your whole heart, right? I deserve to be loved fully. I can't accept half of a heart, no matter who it's from. Half of a heart, even from you, isn't enough for me.

That's not real love."

At a loss for words, I got up from the left side of the couch, walked towards Tee, hugged her while saying, "I totally understand. You and I both know you deserve a whole heart—real love."

Before Tee closed my door, she turned around one final time and embraced me while saying, "Hassan, you can't love anyone until you love yourself enough to heal. What happened wasn't your fault. You have to find a way to accept that."

Once Tasha made her exit, I made my way over to my antique record player and played the only record that could comfort my heart, "Distant Lover." While singing along with Marvin, my mind replayed Tee walking out of my life and towards the altar to marry Darren countless times.

As the memory of the night that Tee announced her engagement dissolved, I drifted back to reality as Dr. Williams repeated her question. "Hassan, what's stopping you from asking Tasha to call off her engagement and pursing the woman that you obviously have deep feelings for?"

As I pondered Dr. Williams' question, my eyes drifted to one of my favorite pictures. To Dr. Williams' right on the mahogany end table rested a picture of my father, Deuce and me. My dad was as dapper as could be in dark blue jeans and a Ralph Lauren Polo, and of course, Deuce and I had on fly attire as well. I remembered that day as if it had occurred yesterday. My dad pulled up in front of the crib bumping Eric B & Rakim's classic song, I ain't No Joke. He leaned on his car and nodded his head from side to side to the classic breakbeat. My dad aggressively nodded his head from side to side with the stink face to convey how fully immersed he was in listening to a legend spit bars of fury. As Rakim rapped about having a question that was as serious as terminal cancer and keeping the crowd hyped, Deuce and I ran out of the house at full speed to greet our dad.

By the time we made it outside, Rakim was spitting a few bars that even Deuce knew. In unison with the legend Rakim, my dad, Deuce and I spit Rakim's incredible lyrics bar for bar.

As Rakim's elite lyrics concluded, my dad gave me a pound while pulling me in for a shoulder hug. And then he lifted Deuce with ease and held him tight before he started sharing his random philosophies about life with us.

"Hassan and Deuce, my pride and joy. The two most incredible young boys in the entire world," he would always state before delving into whatever topic he felt like discussing on a particular day. "My sons, do you know your purpose and mission in life?" I didn't have an answer, so I just remained quiet. But Deuce, who was never at a loss for words, offered his thoughts. Deuce excitedly exclaimed, "stay black and die!" In perplexed fashion, my dad retorted, "You must have heard your funny aunt who likes to drink too many Moscow Mules say that. While there's some truth to that Deuce, our primary mission in life is to protect and love our women. Correction, woman," he stated as he held up his index finger to indicate one woman. "Singular, not plural, guys. Under no circumstances should a man ever fail to provide food and shelter for his family. I don't care how dire life becomes. Under no circumstances should a man fail to protect his wife and family. I don't care if you have to work a job you hate or do time in prison to protect your family. You should always make putting food on the table and protecting your family the number one priority in your life. Deuce, I'm always going to protect you, but if I'm not around for some reason, you can always count on your big brother Hassan to protect you. Ain't that right, H!" he happily and confidently proclaimed.

"You know it Pops, I learned from the best. You can always count on me to protect Deuce, no matter what," I replied as I gave my father a pound and picked Deuce up and spun him around until he was overcome with dizziness.

8

ALL LOVE, NO HATE

Watching and listening intently while my best friend struggled to compose a compelling defense to justify my behavior was starting to take a toll on me. I couldn't tell if Hassan was sabotaging my trial on purpose or if he was just in above his head or perhaps overwhelmed by the opponent he was up against. I suppose nothing in life prepares a lawyer for facing an all-knowing deity that takes on the role of prosecutor, judge and jury. With my soul's fate and final destination hanging in the balance, the best lawyer known to me was running out of time as the judge of all judges easily dismissed and dismantled each argument that Hassan put forth.

Disillusioned by my best friend's inexplicable poor courtroom performance, I sank deeper into my chair and deeper into the abyss of hopelessness. I had survived many trials and tribulations in the streets of Tree Port, but I could feel it in my heart that I was about to go down for a crime that

I didn't feel was worthy of eternal condemnation. The prospect of going to prison for eternity was starting to feel imminent as my hope of being found innocent drifted beyond the horizon of freedom.

When I first arrived in heaven, it took me a while to realize I had passed away in my sleep and that I was officially on trial for taking Hassan's life during my late twenties. Once I realized I would be on trial for ending my best friend's life prematurely, an Eternal Being appeared and informed me that I could either represent myself or have someone speak on my behalf on Judgement Day. I immediately accepted the Eternal Being's offer and requested legal representation. Subsequently, I let it be known that the person whose life I took would be able to explain why my decision to fire my gun on that dreadful day was not murder. No one was better equipped to take on the challenge of defending me than Hassan. I had seen him defy the odds on so many occasions. There was no doubt in my mind that Hassan would rise to the occasion and free my soul on Judgement Day.

Heading into the trial for my soul, I had the utmost confidence that Hassan would make light work of my murder charge. On the day in question, I felt it in my heart that it was necessary to end Hassan's life to prevent an all-out war in Tree Port. I didn't take my best friend's life out of hate or malice; I took it out of necessity. I ended Hassan's life to ensure that so many others would be able to live in peace and to prevent a war with the West End that surely would have erupted if Hassan had lived to see another day.

On Earth, Hassan was undefeated as a defense lawyer. His brilliance knew no boundaries, and he specialized in creating believable and credible narratives that jurors accepted as the truth. His words were as elegant and artistic as a Rembrandt painting. Every case that he accepted sharpened his knowledge of the law and made him more exceptional at his craft. Hassan emerged from his contentious courtroom battles with prosecutors with more confidence and new legal tricks that he would leverage in later battles to sway indecisive jurors. His unique way of articulating his thoughts and deconstructing evidence left judges and juries in disbelief as they would find his clients innocent on all charges. Even when they initially believed and felt that Hassan's clients were as guilty as sin.

On eleven different occasions, I witnessed my childhood friend brilliantly outclass prominent prosecutors with his ingenuity and unparalleled wit. Hassan had a natural knack for leveraging jury members' insecurities in favor of his clients, even when his clients were likely guilty. During jury selection, he never opposed any jurors that the prosecutors preferred. He would just sit back and listen while analyzing each juror's response to the questions he deemed pertinent. Hassan had an interesting philosophical approach to jury selection. He believed lawyers should select questionable jurors instead of rejecting them. His theory was that questionable jurors were more likely to expose their actual biases than potential jurors who carefully curated well-thought-out responses to portray themselves as ideal fits. Hassan believed the power in selecting jurors wasn't in trying to identify open-minded jurors as opened minded people tend to head into trials undecided, which makes it harder to determine which direction they would ultimately vote in on verdict day. He believed bias jurors were more likely to hold firm in their initial positions, but if you managed to convince them that your client was innocent, they would hold firm in voting innocent because their minds weren't easily changed in the first place. In Hassan's mind, people who started trials undecided could be swayed back and forth between guilt and innocence. He would rather have several jurors who were upfront about their biases because it made it easier to determine how to best create and shape narratives that appeal to their sensibilities. As he would always say, "Every human is susceptible to changing their mind when presented with information that fits a narrative they are comfortable with. A carefully crafted story that allows a juror to align their beliefs and thoughts with my clients' actions is an undefeated formula. I just have to figure out which narrative they are most comfortable with and link it to my client's story and innocence. I don't care if a juror is racist because a racist typically doesn't see themselves as a racist. I can leverage the blind loyalty and patriotism that a racist has for their guns and the American flag by making them think that my client has been wronged in the same manner that they feel that liberals have wronged them."

I remember Hassan's very first case like it was yesterday. Fresh out of law school, he represented a client who was charged with an unspeakable and brutal murder. With his first client battling football numbers for a despicable and heinous alleged crime, Hassan did the unthinkable to open his very first trial. He told his client, don't cut your hair, don't shave and don't wear a nice suit to court. As if that advice wasn't incompetent enough, he became the first lawyer in history to show up to the first day of trial, not dressed in a suit and tie. Hassan had the audacity and unmitigated gall to stand before the judge as a defense attorney while wearing jeans and a polo shirt. When Hassan came strolling into the courtroom wearing a Lacoste polo shirt and faded blue jeans, I remember whispering to Tee, "What in the world is wrong with your boy? Hassan has lost his mind. Is he trying to get disbarred?" As if the foolish wisdom that prompted him to dress like he was going to a nightclub instead of a courtroom wasn't astonishing enough. Hassan proudly advised his client to wear his oversized orange prison jumpsuit on the first day of trial.

Tee and the rest of my Tree Port comrades who were there to support Hassan just sat there pondering if H had lost his mind. Flabbergasted court attendees took huge gasps and uttered comments such as: "The convict should just renounce his lawyer and defend himself. Did this lawyer even pass the Bar?" and countless other insults that certainly appeared to be warranted at the time.

As the judge gazed at Hassan in disbelief, he permitted the prosecuting attorney to make their opening argument. Astonished by Hassan's approach, I whispered to Tee, "Our boy wasted over ninety-thousand dollars on law school to become the worst lawyer ever? H and I go way back to the sandbox. He's one of my day one homies, but I would fire him on the spot," I quipped jokingly, even though I wasn't joking. "Prince, maybe he's nervous. His nerves may be getting the best of him. Let's have a quick chat with him as soon as the judge grants a recess," replied a concerned Tee. I nodded my head in agreement and told Tee I agreed that we definitely should try to calm Hassan down during the upcoming recess.

As Tee and I solidified our plan to save Hassan from further embarrassing himself, something beyond belief occurred. What happened next? You had to be present in the courtroom that day to believe it. After wrapping up their opening statement the prosecutor confidently took a seat in the brown wooden chair before the judge and jury that seemed supremely impressed by their argument. Once the prosecutor was seated a buoyant Hassan draped in a yellowish Lacoste shirt, and fitted blue jeans kicked off his initial rebuttal. Instantly, he began to show glimpses of what made him special. The sparkling glimmer of brilliance that Tee and I knew was somewhere deep inside Hassan was shining as bright as the Orion and dwarfing the cloud of doubt that we once had as Hassan lit the courtroom up with stars of genius. He proved he was already a legal maven to be reckoned with, and the scary thing was, he was just getting started.

"My client and I are dressed in casual clothing today because we don't take these malicious, ill-advised charges and allegations seriously. Too often, we see guilty criminals and lawyers who are fully aware of their clients' guilt advise their clients to become something different from what they have been their whole life. Cut your hair, put on a nice suit and tie to present yourself as a clean-cut male who's perfect and incapable of ever committing a crime in life. My client will engage in no such illusion-based forgery of his character. He's adorned in the orange jumpsuit provided by our *wonderful* prison system because he has been to prison before, and he's been a prisoner in this country his entire life. He's the slave that the Emancipation Proclamation didn't free. He didn't have an opportunity to flee north for a better life. Instead, he was trapped and denied the chance to use his entrepreneurial ingenuity in a way that society deems legal. He committed acts that are similar to those on Wall Street that caused the economy to crash, but since he's not on Wall Street, he was shunned and condemned for his actions instead of being bailed out by the government and jokingly shamed with a slap on the wrist like those in the good ole boy club. He has owned up to his guilt for every crime he has committed in the past by pleading guilty. Today is the only time that he has decided to plead not guilty. What does that tell you? He has committed crimes before, and he isn't ashamed of his past, as his past is what inspired him to change his life for the better.

"He refused to cut his dreadlocks because he believes there is power in his hair as Sampson did. If you are intimidated by my client's attire, tattoos, or hair, it says more about you than it does about him. How would you feel if I were intimidated by you and opposed your right to bear arms? How would you feel if you weren't able to be yourself? If you had to conceal your gun and who you are as a person in the hopes that others would see you for the individual you really are, would you be okay with that? Judge not, lest you be judged. When you look at my client, it is ok for you to see a criminal. A hardened criminal is what he used to be. Today you are looking at what my client used to be—a prisoner of an unfair and unjust system that doesn't afford everyone the same opportunities to succeed and enjoy the American Dream. The orange jumpsuit and the handcuffs on his wrist can confine him as if he's guilty of murder, but those same handcuffs cannot and will not imprison his mind. During this trial, I will provide extensive details that explain what my client is capable of. He's capable and incapable of the same things that each person on this jury is capable of. Are you capable of murdering someone over a trivial disagreement? My client is capable of being frustrated and extremely upset, but his anger would never drive him to violate the ultimate commandment, "Thou Shall Not Kill." He's a God-fearing man who fell off the horse as Saul did on the road to Damascus when he saw the light. He course-corrected to become a better person. If my client is capable of murder, that means you are capable of murder. Because, just like you, he is a hard-working individual who respects and values the lives of others. He would never fire a bullet that takes life for granted. He never killed anyone during his wildest days, so why would this man who used his last stint in prison to grow as a person become certified as an electrician and plumber randomly decide to kill someone for no reason? What we are witnessing is an unconscionable miscarriage of justice. My client would not and did not commit a murder that you wouldn't commit. You aren't capable of taking a life, and he isn't capable of taking a life either."

On that day in the courtroom, the morning of Hassan's very first trial, I started to understand the foolish wisdom that resided in him. H and I go way back. We first met as toddlers as our fathers were good friends and brought us around one another before we could even speak or mutter real words. My friendship with Hassan was tried and true. A lifelong bond that embers of loyalty had forged as the result of surviving so many Tree Port street fires together.

While there were many occasions where we had heated disagreements, I can only recall one instance where we almost came to blows. One day at the blacktop basketball court, we were on opposing teams, and things got somewhat contentious on what should have been the game-winning basket for the final game. A few minutes before the streetlights were due to come on and send us home per our moms' *streetlights are on* curfew, I dribbled past Hassan and made what I presumed to be the game-winning layup. As excitement erupted from my squad at the prospect of beating the Santino-led team that Hassan was part of, Hassan casually stated, "Prince, ball up top. I got you on the wrist." While it was true that H had hit my arm as I was driving towards the hoop, I didn't call the foul. The onus was typically on the offensive player to call the foul and everyone in Tree Port abided by the philosophy that if the foul didn't draw blood, it was play on.

"H, come on. You bugging bro, that's game. I ain't call no foul."

"Nah, Prince, you tripping. You know I slowed up

because I fouled you early on that drive with the expectation that it would be ball out up top. Fam, run that point back."

"I'm not running nothing back. We just won. Game over," I declared angrily.

Santino sensed that things were escalating quickly and getting out of hand. Tino tried to quell the tension between Hassan and me by saying, "Prince, it's all good. The streetlights are about to come on anyway. Hassan, let them have this one. We'll run it back tomorrow, and you have my word that we won't lose," he stated. Santino extended his left hand towards me and his right hand towards Hassan for a courtesy pound to confirm that we were on board with his words and arbitration. Instead of responding with a pound, Hassan and I left Santino hanging as our anger with one another continued to simmer.

Santino playing peacemaker would normally cool things down and force cooler heads to prevail. But a cordial departure from the court wasn't in the cards on that fateful evening as the sun dawned and the streetlights lit up our legendary blacktop court. Hassan wasn't budging on conceding the game, and I was refusing to run the final sequence of the game back. The tension between Hassan and me continued to escalate. Until Hassan and I eventually started circling one another with our fists clutched tightly. As we angrily circled one another while waiting to see if the other person would swing, our shoulders clashed a time or two while we blew hot air in each other's faces. As we huffed and puffed in anger and circled one another slowly, Hassan's cousin Marcus had the genius idea to take two broken sticks and place them on our shoulders. "The stick that I put on Hassan's shoulder is our dead great-grandma, and the stick on your shoulder is your dead grandma Prince," stated the agitator, who was anxious for a fight to pop off. Anytime a fight was taking too long to kick off in Tree Port, you could always count on an agitator to place two broken sticks on the offended parties' shoulders. Marcus, the notorious agitator in the crew, was anxious to see if Hassan or I would be bold enough to disrespect the other person's deceased family member by knocking the stick off the other person's shoulder.

As the sky grew darker and we continued to circle one another, Marcus bumped into me with the hopes of knocking the stick, which symbolized my beloved and deceased grandma to the ground. As I stumbled forward after the not so accidental bump from Marcus, my grandma lost her balance and tumbled from my shoulder as the urgency of gravity beckoned her towards the ground. Luckily, as the stick that represented my deceased grandmother was nearing the grass, Hassan's respect for my Grandma Nina caused him to intervene. As my grandma fell from my shoulder and drifted closer to the dirt, Hassan utilized his quick reflexes to catch

Grandma Nina before she hit the earth. Hassan's immediate reaction and respect for my grandma prevented what surely would have been a never-ending fight had my grandma fell to the ground. If we had fought that day, the Nothing to Lose crew might have been fractured forever, but instead of a fight; Hassan stopped circling me and handed me the stick that represented my grandma and said, "Santino's right, the streetlights are on Prince, I gotta head home." I was relieved that Hassan and I didn't come to blows that day. When I fight, I fight to the death, and that's why I don't fight often. Words lead to fights; fights lead to guns, and guns lead to wars. And in war, there are casualties. That's why I always preferred peace over war. I would never be able to live with myself if my actions led to a war that cost someone's life from my block. I loved my brothers dearly, and I wanted them to live forever.

9

WHAT THE COINTELPRO CAN'T STOP

We were one of the few blocks in Tree Port that had gone years without losing a member of our crew to gun violence. All of the other sides, the West End, the north side and the south side, had all suffered tragic losses. Many of the losses that the other crews suffered could have been prevented if people had set aside their egos and learned to communicate instead of always jumping to the conclusion that a gun was the best orator. I considered my block lucky and blessed. We didn't have many hotheads, and we moved strategically for the most part.

I became the de facto leader of the Nothing to Lose crew at a relatively young age. Our block was different from other hoods in Tree Port. We didn't have an official chief, leader, or shot-caller who could tell or demand that other crew members carry out acts of violence just because the Chief said so. Unlike the hoods that surrounded us, we didn't send our brothers out on dummy missions at the behest of a so-called OG that was afraid to do his own dirt. If you had drama with someone, it was your responsibility and yours alone to stand on business. Instead of the typical hierarchy where the OGs or the person with the most money ordered other crew members around, we operated like what America claims to be, a real democracy. For the people by the people, for the hood by the hood. Everyone in our crew was truly equal; there was no distorted electoral college voting that allowed for the dismissal of popular voting results.

When the respect that the crew had for me blossomed to a level that made me the de facto leader, I recommended principles of peace and standards of restraint that the crew as a whole felt comfortable adopting. Central to my beliefs was the idea that violence should be the last resort and only carried out if it would help prevent an all-out war. Another core principle of mine was that our hood needed to refrain from selling drugs to generate income. Drugs had an overall net negative impact on the community that no amount of money could ever make up for. Also, drug sentences were overly harsh. In addition to understanding that the ROI from drug profits wasn't worth the harsh prison sentences, I understood that time was a gift that we could never get back once it's lost. I was uncomfortable with the damage that drugs did to my people. I had seen the lingering effects of drug usage up close and personal as Big Momma was a saint on Sunday but a trapper Monday – Saturday. Growing up, I spent a lot of time at Big Momma's trap house.

My grandma was a jack of all trades and a master of accumulating profits. Like JFK's father, she was a bootlegger extraordinaire, except she had an assortment of products for sale. Her inventory wasn't relegated to just liquor. Big Momma sold it all. She sold loose cigarettes, candy to kids, liquor by the cup, pills to addicts and whatever else was making the rounds in Tree Port at the time. On most Saturdays, Big Momma shut the trap down early because she needed her rest to make sure she was up early enough to teach Sunday school at church. One particular Saturday night, I remember her instructing my uncle to keep the spot open an additional hour. I remember her yelling at my uncle, "Howard, don't double-bolt that door just yet! I got enough money to pay the bills, but I need another sixty dollars to make sure I got my ten percent for the Lord tomorrow. God ain't blessing this trap for nothing. As for me and my house, we gon' serve the Lord and pay our tithes too," she stated while puffing on her Newport that looked like it was about to fall from her lip at any moment. It was probably time for her to let that cigarette go as it was littered with more grey ashes than it had white wrapper paper remaining. How she was able to hang on to her Newports with just her bottom lip while she talked and gave so many orders is a mystery that I will never know the answer to.

Being present during those times taught me a great deal. It taught me that even if you are in a poor environment, people still gravitate towards capitalism and dismiss elements of socialism because they have been conditioned to believe that someday they will be at the top of the food chain. And when they reach the top, they don't intend to share much with those at the bottom. For some reason, everyone believes that they deserve to be rich one day and that others deserve to remain poor because they didn't "work as hard as them," whatever that means. Just like my grandma, I understood people, money and the intentions of the cops. One of the primary goals that I had for my crew was to stay off the radar of the cops.

The Nothing to Lose crew was the only group of young black males in Tree Port that wasn't classified as a gang by the Tree Port PD gang task force. Not being classified as a gang was a critical distinction that everyone in our crew worked hard to maintain. Being classified as a gang could lead to conspiracy and RICO charges that could easily land an entire crew in prison. We saw it happen to so many gangs in our areas. In the interest of avoiding prison at all cost, our squad was dedicated to being different from all the other cliques that existed in Tree Port. We didn't carry out unprovoked acts of violence. We didn't rock specific colors, and we didn't flash gang signs or claim our affiliation on social media. In fact, no one outside of our crew knew what to refer to us as. We were akin to the black hand on the Godfather movie cover; silent and unseen but pulling substantial strings behind the scenes. Other blocks often called us Prince's crew or Santino's crew, which was cool with us. Unbeknownst to the rival blocks that surrounded our hood, the Nothing to Lose name was actually derived from the legendary basketball games at the blacktop court. To make things fair, we had these revolving teams where players from our hood would rotate from being on Santino's squad to the team playing against Santino, i.e., the losing team. Santino's team was so likely to win every game that we called the group of players that ended up on the opposing team the Nothing to Lose crew. At the end of the day, what do you have to lose if you always lose to the team led by a nationally ranked player? Absolutely nothing because you never win anyway.

Back then, I had no blueprint to follow as I worked to construct guidelines and principles that would make our crew a net positive instead of a net negative to the community. I studied the Black Panthers. I researched SNCC, spoke to OG's like my dad, and had multiple conversations with Hassan's dad when I realized that the Nothing to Lose crew was a movement that extended beyond just being a basketball team. As I was spending time crafting principles and morals that I thought our block would benefit from, I received a letter from my cousin Quise. Quise grew up in the Gashouse and became a History major who enjoyed traveling the world and thinking about ways to improve communities. While he was in the Motherland, the home of Haile Selassie, to be exact, he sent me a letter shaped like an Ethiopian Pyramid that outlined a movement that he was commissioning.

He was developing a movement dedicated to creating a shared consciousness and understanding amongst our people. He opened his letter with a greeting and then immediately stated, "My feelings, thoughts and actions regarding my people will be rooted in All Love, No Hate."

In his letter, he outlined the following:

Quise explained why African Americans needed to demand reparations from the United States government immediately.

In his words, reparations were not optional. Reparations were a demand that must be met by the government and any politicians that wish to secure votes from African Americans.

"Prince, use your voice and platform to spread the message that we refuse to vote for politicians who don't support reparations in the form of direct payments," he implored in his letter. "We must take a stance that can't be swayed by threats that this is the most important election of our lifetimes or deflections that now is not the right time to discuss reparations. That's a trap to get us to defer pursuing our birthright, a diversion to get us to forget the 40 acres and a mule that was promised to us more than a century ago."

He also stated that we needed to draw a line in the sand. In his words, "Anyone who opposes reparations is a supporter of systemic oppression and racism, that's non-negotiable. We demand reparations now!"

In his letter, he detailed how egregious it is for African Americans to pay taxes to a country that owes us reparations. "We are essentially indentured servants. We can't pretend to be free while the country that owes us trillions of dollars takes money out of our paychecks. Can you believe we pay taxes in a country that owes us reparations? Unbelievable and utterly unacceptable."

He also stated that he would provide his account and routing number to African Americans who opposed reparations. "I'll tell you what, for those that oppose reparations, I'll take their portion. It's funny to me that those that kick bootstrap rhetoric and proclaim to oppose handouts are always talking about the importance of generation wealth while openly opposing what's owed to us. I suppose those same individuals would be one-hundred percent comfortable with working hard all of their lives to accumulate wealth and not being able to pass down a dime of their earned savings to their children. Since they oppose reparations, shouldn't they be against passing wealth down via inheritances as well?

In support of his thoughts on reparations, he launched a website called wedemandreparationsnow.com.

After Quise finished outlining his thoughts on reparations, he ventured into explaining the core principles of the All Love, No Hate initiative.

My goals and dreams are for our people to develop a shared consciousness rooted in love as a means of improving our predicament and conditions.

It starts and ends with "I shall not commit any acts of violence against my brothers or sisters under any circumstances. All disputes will be resolved with love and understanding. If a disagreement turns hostile and cannot be resolved for any reason, I agree to walk away as a means to protect myself, my brothers and sisters.

"I will not harbor or support members of the community that commit acts of violence against the innocent. I will demand that perpetrators who harm the innocent accept responsibility for their actions. If they refuse to do so, I will turn them in myself.

"As men in our community, we must decide if we are finally going to stand up. Are we going to continue to allow the criminal element, the minority in the community, to make the rules? Are we going to continue to accept that anything goes? Little kids and elderly people being shot currently has no consequences or repercussions. Because you and I, and many others who claim to care about the community, have turned a blind eye to the lives that have been lost. How long are we going to allow the wrong people to make the rules in our community? Those of us who care about the community should be the ones crafting and determining what the principles are for our blocks. And those morals and principles should be for the betterment and protection of all who want to live peaceful and safe lives.

"When attempting to speak on a complicated issue, I will not rely on flawed logic or memes that are rooted in demeaning our people. If the point that I'm attempting to make can be traced back to a racist trope or talking point, I will examine how I'm framing the issue and explore the self-hate components that are within me that prompted me to craft my point in a manner that disparages my people.

"I will do my best to educate myself on complicated topics before making declarations that are cliché reliant and not rooted in facts.

"I will acknowledge when I'm wrong, and I will respect valid counter-arguments and perspectives that prompt me to grow my way of thinking."

Self-Hate Eradication:

"The one thing that America taught us to do well is to hate ourselves. Self-hate materializes in a myriad of ways: negative thoughts about ourselves, agreement with racists sentiments, and ultimately, unnecessary acts of violence. We are taught on a conscious and subconscious level that being black is inferior, which informs our perspectives on a plethora of issues. Just think quickly about some of the clichés and views that we may have believed at some point and how pervasive and rampant the belief in them are.

"Black people don't support black businesses is a popular negative sentiment that is espoused by many. The notion that black people don't support black businesses is typically a projection. Frequently, it means, "I don't support black businesses; therefore, I'm comfortable making the leap and assumption that most African Americans don't support black businesses. How can this be true? Number one, if we don't support black businesses, how are the successful ones surviving? Does our non-support of black companies extend to churches, barbershops, hair salons, etc., just to name a few? Those businesses seem to be thriving and doing well, but what do I know?

"Similarly, the belief that black people will spend money on luxury brands but won't support their own is deeply flawed. Before buying into this assumption, take the time to do a quick mental survey of your family, friends and associates' spending habits. How many of them own an article of clothing or an accessory from the luxury brand that you claim that African Americans support over black businesses? Not many, I bet!

"Now that we have covered our support of black businesses, I want to touch on another misnomer. The myth that we are inherently more violent than others. It is a logical fallacy to believe that we control and own the burden of the violent actions of a small minority of individuals that share our complexion. Based on our shared skin color and some cultural similarities, we belong to a general black community, but we do not have the power, knowledge, or ability to control the street politics of every black neighborhood. Communities that we don't reside in have nuances, street politics and systemic oppression vestiges that we may not be familiar with that contribute to violence.

"Prince, in closing, I'm challenging you, Acton, Jefe da Boss, E Bills, Malcolm, Mike, Devin McCullough, Quintin Young, Brian Thompson, Travis Pagan, Ray Money, Ryan Howell, Majid, Slim, Josh, Deion, Trubb and Ric James to utilize your intellectual dexterity, talents and actions to improve and protect our communities.

"Prince, I wish you and the Nothing to Lose crew well, and I implore you to implement a strict policy that prohibits acts of violence from your squad. To truly be dangerous, one must lay the gun to rest and unlock the hidden wisdom that resides in the heart and mind. The most dangerous threat to the world is an educated brother who gravitates towards his soul's wisdom and love. Our souls are rooted in All Love, No

Hate.

Peace King,

Blessings and love from your favorite father and son duo, Quise and Josiah and of course, my wife, Jalisa."

After I finished reading Quise's letter, I sat silently and contemplated why he always sent long letters instead of just emailing me. Must be the History major in him, I thought to myself.

10

DO WE HATE OUR WOMEN?

W hile reflecting on the advice and words in the letter that I received from Quise, I reminisced about simpler times; my adolescent years when OGs had real influence over the youth and actually cared about the lives of the up and coming generation. During my formative years, I spent a lot of time in the streets of Tree Port and during those days, the Nothing to Lose crew and the surrounding hoods had a tremendous amount of respect and admiration for the older generation that paved the way for us. The OGs taught us to be kind to the elderly, to refrain from using vulgar language around young ladies and kids, and most importantly, to take pride in being Black. Those days were long gone, and all signs pointed to those times never returning. Concerned OGs no longer patrolled the blocks to offer sound advice that steered youngsters in the right direction. The hood's concerned elder statesmen were replaced by unorganized loudmouth leaders and know-it-all imbeciles who were the same age as those following them. And those know-it-all imbeciles took pride in igniting random beefs on social media that ultimately got youngsters from their blocks killed. The connectivity that existed across generations during my youth had evaporated from my hood. Individuals who didn't care about anyone but themselves had managed to fill the void of the missing OGs by being loud and willing to shoot anybody they disagreed with.

When I was growing up, OG Prince and the other shot callers from my block actively taught us street laws, how to interact with cops, rules of engagement as it pertains to resolving conflict, and how to conduct ourselves in a manner that minimized violence. I remember being on the block with my pops while Marvin Gaye's lyrics blared from his car speaker. As I looked at my father in admiration, Marvin crooned about wanting love the right way and his desire for love to be reciprocated the right way. As Marvin Gaye delivered his incredible lyrics, a decent-sized crowd began to congregate around my dad. OG Prince had the type of presence that reeled people into his orbit organically. He was naturally smooth without even trying; a suave and debonair renaissance man if you will.

On that particular day, my dad was draped in Vinny McFly attire designed by Kim Davis from head to toe and swaying back and forth to the elegant instrumental that Marvin sung "I Want You" over. When my father started talking, the residents of Tree Port would gather around to listen as he shared invaluable gems with those in attendance. Everyone from my block seemed to enjoy hearing my father's perspective on a myriad of subjects. Whenever OG Prince was kind enough to bless the block with his presence, the top drug dealers, killers with no conscience and young kids who liked to hoop would gather around and listen intently. Surrounded by black and white 5.0 Mustang drug dealer cars adorned with gold Dayton rims and those interested in learning something new, my father would start by asking an interesting question and then let his wisdom flow like the Nile.

"Prince, why do you think so many people own guns in America?" he asked while observing the crowd and giving everyone in attendance a stern look that indicated his question was directed at his son and required no interjections or input from the crowd.

"Pops, I don't know. Maybe people own guns to protect themselves and their families, I guess," I replied.

"Son, close, but no cigar," my dad replied as he shook his head while chuckling at my response. "People in America own so many guns because they have been conditioned to fear their neighbors and have been rewarded for not valuing others' lives as much as their own. When you pick up a gun and discharge a bullet to take a life, you are in essence saying to God; I'm better equipped to determine when this person's life should end than the Most High is. Prince, violence should always be the last resort, especially when handling disputes in your own community. I don't care how well the NRA markets weapons to the general public. Guns don't exist to resolve problems; guns live to end lives. Always remember that son."

I missed being able to safely post on the block like that with my dad. Cool enjoyable evenings when adults decked in their best attire, pulled up to the block blasting classic songs and excitedly hopped out of their newly washed cars and proceeded to greet everyone present with love and hugs. Yesterdays like that only existed in my memories and would never return. Violence was the default now. No one gave a flying **** about having a good time or talking things out to prevent drama from spiraling out of control. If drama popped off, someone was getting shot or killed as a result. Nobody in our crew or the other crews even knew where to start an effort to broker peace amongst the younger crews in Tree Port. Decades ago, 2Pac said, "There can never be peace," and he was right.

While there was a significant divide in how my crew conducted ourselves compared to the younger crews in Tree Port, we shared a mutual understanding with some of the more sensible crews. While the younger generation in Tree Port never reached out to form an official alliance with my crew due to our strict guidelines; they did respect us enough to abide by our principles when in our territory. One time, someone from the younger generation interrupted one of our basketball games and asked us to listen to a young rapper spit some bars. The up-and-coming rapper needed our co-sign and permission to rep the block in his music.

After listening to the youngster rap for one or two minutes, I asked, "Why do your lyrics revolve around killing and violence so much? I like your flow and lyrical dexterity, but no one in our crew is going to co-sign or embrace a lyricist who constantly raps about killing and destroying other black men so much. Have you ever consider expanding your content or being a bit more creative?"

The young rapper brashly interjected, "This is the type of music the people want to hear OG. It's just entertainment. I'm just giving the people what they want. A true depiction of the streets. Stories about our hood that allows those from the suburbs to safely visit where we are from for three minutes. I'm rapping about life as I know it. I'm rapping about what I know and what I see every day."

"Kid, trust me. I understand rapping about your environment, and I'm not telling you to sugarcoat the truth, but at some point, it's overkill. The diminishing returns aren't worth the negative energy you are inviting into your life with these violent lyrics. If you proclaim from the mountain top that you are the toughest and most vicious king of the jungle, don't be shocked or alarmed when the hyenas in the valley test your gangster and eventually come for your crown. Over the course of two minutes, you shot and killed nine people in your rhymes. Am I watching Bruce Willis kill his enemies in Die Hard, or am I just listening to a rapper destined to die hard? Also, are you sure your content is truly what the people want? One thousand rappers are rapping about selling drugs and harming other brothers, and most of them don't sell a significant number of records. The way the radio plays these records, you would think violent rappers would be the highest sellers, but they aren't. None of these rappers who constantly talk about killing other black men can sell the number of records that J. Cole and Kendrick Lamar sell. These drill rappers are a dime a dozen. And these record labels are leveraging them for a quick dollar because that type of artist is extremely easy to manufacture. These record labels don't care when the music being created causes more murders in the hoods that these rappers are from. Record executives and their companies are complicit contributors to the violence that music is inciting in the streets."

I pointed at the young man to emphasize my next point and stated, "You have to ask yourself, why do you hate yourself so much that you feel it is appropriate to rhyme about shooting and killing other black men constantly? To acquire support from this crew, you need to grow as a rapper, expand your content and perspective. If you are truly interested in growing as an artist and developing and honing your skills, I can put you in contact with my talented musical friends Notca and Black Talon. The choice is yours."

After my long soliloquy, the rapper from the younger generation brushed my words off and headed in the opposite direction.

That's the story of my life. In so many instances, I tried everything within my power to save others from imminent danger. Danger that they seemed blind to, a danger they seemed determined to run towards instead of from. It took me a long time to realize that you can't save people from destruction if death and violence are what they are attracted to. Hassan, my best friend, wasn't any different. While Hassan wasn't drawn to destruction per se, he had experienced a loss or two that he never learned to live with, which sometimes impacted his ability to thoroughly think things through before acting, which in turn put him and those close to him in harm's way.

I remember having a conversation with Hassan about the violence in Tree Port after he pulled his gun on Renlo during the meeting of the minds.

"Hassan, what's the point of having a meeting of the minds if we aren't going to use our minds? Guns are one of the reasons why our community is littered with violence right now. How can a gun be the question and the answer? How can your pistol be the problem and the solution?" I inquired.

Hassan stared off into the distance for a few moments as he processed my words. "Prince, you're right. That was my bad. I put us in a terrible predicament during the meeting of the minds," he stated as he pondered what to say next.

"Prince, you ever do something that you know is inherently wrong despite knowing it's wrong while you're doing it? But for some strange reason, you can't stop yourself even though you know it's the wrong move to make?"

I shook my head in agreement to acknowledge that I could relate to Hassan's point about making mistakes. Speaking of wrongdoing, I had committed the ultimate wrong when I took Hassan's life. Pulling a gun out and using it on my best friend shattered my heart into pieces that would never form a full heart again. It was the most challenging decision that I ever made. I was never the same after taking Hassan's life. While I felt that my actions were a necessary evil, I never found a way to live or cope with my decision. From the moment the bullet recoiled and exited the chamber, I always wondered what life would have been like for me and the Nothing to Lose Crew if I had found a different way to resolve the conflict brewing between Hassan and Renlo. What if I could rewind time? What if before Hassan took his last breath, the bullet that I fired emerged from his cranium and erased the smoke from the gun that Hassan smelled a millisecond before the bullet penetrated the first centimeter of his skin? What if that lone bullet traveled back into the barrel entrance of my gun and returned to the chamber while my index finger released the trigger, and the firearm settled back to being still in the air. What if my pistol never jolted upward because the murderous bullet that I fired was never fired? What if I had thought long and hard enough to find a different solution to prevent an all-out war in Tree Port? What if the path of how bullets and guns ended up in our possession and incited genocide were fully understood by me and my cohorts in Tree Port?

If time had a guilty conscience and could rewind itself, would time decide to go in reverse and erase the ideas of Chinese alchemists that blended charcoal, saltpeter and sulfur into a powder called huo yao? If time was awake, would it travel in reverse and kill off all individuals seeking to refine gun powder recipes? Perhaps time wouldn't change a thing if it could. Because time probably understands that humans always find a new and creative way to kill each other anyway. Perhaps if time had a conscience, it would erase the terrible day that Hassan died from my memory. Unfortunately, time has no guilty conscience.

I remember that dreadful day like it was yesterday. The

day that I decided to cut my best friend's life short. The day that I became a monster who would never smile again when looking at his reflection in the mirror. The day that I cried tears that God didn't catch. Early that morning, Tee hit my line to let me know that she was very concerned about Hassan. She explained how Hassan wasn't in his right frame of mind and how he was determined to kill Renlo no matter what.

While I understood why Hassan felt that Renlo must die, I knew it was too big of a risk for our crew to kill a well-respected gang chief. The drama between Renlo and Hassan hit its zenith during the meeting of the minds years ago when Hassan pulled his gun on that chump. Hassan's dad always told him and anyone who would listen, never pull your weapon on a sucker unless you plan to send him to his maker immediately. Hassan always believed and followed whatever advice his dad gave him to the tee, but for some reason, on that day, he ignored the wise words of wisdom that his dad had raised him to believe. A few years after the meeting of the minds fiasco, Renlo went down for a crime that landed him a substantial amount of prison time. But now, he was back on the streets after his second-degree murder bid, and his presence was haunting Hassan. Determined to prevent Renlo from causing further harm in Tree Port, Hassan became obsessed with killing him. Hassan and I had several discussions about how violence begets violence, and I did my best to convince him that killing Renlo would do more harm than good. For all the flaws that Renlo possessed, loyalty to and from his set was not one. He was extremely loyal to his crew, and in return, his clique was forever loyal to him. If the Nothing to Lose Crew decided to take Renlo out, we would be in for a never-ending war with the West End.

"Hassan, you can't just murder a gang chief and expect no blowback. That would be like the West End murdering me. What would the Nothing to Lose clique do if that happened?" I asked.

"Ohhhh, so the Nothing to Lose crew has a chief now?" a stunned Hassan replied as he tilted his head to the right in disgust. "Prince, I didn't know we functioned like these other dumb crews out here. I thought we were what America proclaims to be, a true democracy. For the people by the people, for the hood by the hood. When did one person's opinion, in particular, your opinion start mattering more than the perspectives of others in our squad? I guess it's appropriate that your name is Prince. Because today, you crowned yourself the uncontested king of our crew."

Shocked by Hassan's interpretation of my intent and words, we both just sat there and embraced the quietness and patiently waited for the other person to shatter the glacier of silence that was dividing us. As we sat there in silence, I contemplated Hassan's perspective and surmised that his concerns about Renlo were valid.

Approximately five minutes of pure quietness elapsed before Hassan finally decided to continue our contentious conversation.

"Prince, I don't understand why you think constantly offering peace is the best way to deal with gangsters. Realistically speaking, what are you going to tell a bunch of gangsters who believe in their guns more than they believe in God? These cowards with automatic weapons shoot and kill kids with no remorse. They have no fear. Some of these cats have smoked multiple people without thinking twice about it. Why are you trying to negotiate peace accords with serial killers? One day you're going to realize that some people are so far gone and jaded by their environment and circumstances that the little conscience they were born with evaporated the moment they clutched a trigger for the first time. Prince, you can't save everybody. But you already know that, don't you?" Hassan asked as his eyes drifted towards my immaculate marble floor. The pain in Hassan's eyes reflected off the transparent marble floor with specs of grey in it and proceeded to bounce off the mirror positioned behind him before heading in my direction. Eventually, the pain in Hassan's eyes landed on my shoulder and transformed into a nagging Imp. An Imp that refused to leave my shoulder until I acknowledged the agony that so many people in Tree Port had experienced at the hands of violence.

Deeply frustrated by my dissonance and unwillingness to bend, Hassan propped his head against his open right hand for support and unveiled a trump card. "Prince, have you ever experienced a loss so profound that you know in your heart that no matter how hard you try, you will never be the same? A loss so heartbreaking that you know your heart will never be whole again?"

As Hassan's words of anguish echoed in my head, I reflected on the day that I experienced my most significant loss. That day outside of the Tree Port Community Center when I reacted fast enough to save myself, but not quickly enough to save another person who unfortunately passed away. If I could rewind the hands of time and react differently by giving up my life to save the innocent life that was lost, I would. Some kids are too young and precious to die. Some kids don't deserve death at an early age. Some kids have an indescribable smile and presence that brings joy to the world. Some kids have a future that's so bright it feels wrong when God allows a bullet with no name on it to warp their barely lived lives into mourned memories. At times I felt like I cared more about the youth in Tree Port than God did. If God truly cares, why does it seem like he's oblivious to our pain at times? I guess we will never know. As I pondered one of the most painful days of my life, it was as if Hassan was thinking of that same excruciating day as the tears that God refused to catch formed in our eyes.

Sensing a scintilla of an opening, a final chance to change my mind about ridding the world of Renlo, the undefeated and best lawyer I've ever known, drove home his emotional and poignant closing argument. "Prince, I don't want anyone else in Tree Port to experience the type of loss that we took. Do you?"

I could tell that if I didn't reverse course on ridding the world of Renlo, Hassan was going to spiral to a place of no return. A place where his desire for vengeance would drive him madder than he already was. Before that day, Hassan and I had several conversations about how to handle the West End. Every time we discussed the West End, our conversation ended in an angry stalemate. But this time, it was different. In good conscience, I could not ignore the enormity of the pain that Hassan was living with. Sensing that there was no talking Hassan down after our conversation, I convinced him that I had a solution for dealing with the West End and Renlo. I offered Hassan some Scotch, asked him to trust me, and implored him to stay put no matter what.

My wise and seldom wrong father, OG Prince, had taught me that violence against another brother should always be the last resort. And this was the last resort. All other viable options had been exhausted. No alternative would give

Hassan peace of mind, a path to move beyond the pain of the past and potentially find a new passageway that led to some form of joy. I had to kill Renlo to save my best friend from himself. Medusa's eyes froze my decision to kill Renlo; it was set in stone.

11

TEARS THAT GOD DIDN'T CATCH

U pon leaving Hassan where he was, I called Tee and asked for a huge favor.

"Tee, do you have time to come get me and drive me somewhere real quick?"

"Of course. Prince, you know I got you. I'll see you in fifteen minutes," Tee replied with no hesitation.

I didn't call on Tee often, but whenever I did, she always dropped whatever she was doing to accommodate my requests. There were two things that I could always count on in life: taxes and Tee having my back during difficult times.

When Tee arrived, her Inspector Gadget investigation skills immediately noticed the matte black twenty-two tethered to my waist. After noticing my gun, she started shaking her head as if she was in fear and stated, "I always knew this day would come. Prince, you are going to try to bully me into marrying Hassan instead of Darren, aren't you?" she joked as she tossed her head back in laughter. Tee always knew how to make everybody laugh and smile, even during the darkest of times. I just shook my head from side to side as I slid into the passenger seat of her car.

Tee's engagement to Darren shocked everyone in our crew, but it didn't surprise me. Tasha wasn't the type of woman who would wait forever for Hassan to fully appreciate her, no matter how much she cared about him. I remember a conversation that Tee and I had about Hassan and love before she got engaged. She showed up at my office one day and asked me if I had a few minutes to spare.

"Tee, my day is booked solid, but for you, I can carve out a few minutes. You seem parched. Would you like a glass of water?" I asked as she gathered her thoughts while pacing back and forth. Without speaking, she waved off my offer of water and continued to stroll from one side of my office to the other. While waiting for Tee to unleash the reservoir of thoughts that led to her surprise office visit, I analyzed stock market trends. As Tee marched to and fro like a madwoman on a mission, I purchased call options for an up-and-coming company that I believed would be a major player in the electric car marketplace one day.

Eventually, Tee's back and forth pacing across my office led to huffing and puffing, which subsequently prompted her to take a seat. Once she settled into her chair, she promptly removed her Eleanor Anukam high heels to grant her tired feet some much-needed reprieve. After breathing deeply and relaxing for a few moments, Tee exclaimed, "Prince, guess what? I think Darren is going to ask me to marry him soon."

Upon hearing this shocking revelation, I immediately jumped up from my black leather office chair and hugged her while shouting, "Congratulations! This is amazing. Tee, you deserve all the happiness in the world, and I'm extremely excited for you. Darren is a great guy, and I know he will continue to treat you like the queen that you are," I stated while nodding my head in approval.

As I nestled back into my office chair, I became perplexed by Tee's lack of excitement. "Tasha, what's really good? You just shared the biggest news of your life, yet you don't seem all that excited about your pending engagement."

After a few moments of contemplative stillness, Tee responded to my question with a question. "Prince, have you ever been in a relationship with someone that you know is right for you but still occasionally wondered about a future with a person that you know is wrong for you?"

With no hesitation, I stated, "Tee, can't say that I have. I abide by the principle of loving who loves me and desiring who desires me. Tasha, you have to figure out why you are preoccupied with someone who doesn't want to be with you; when you should be focused on building something special with the person who loves being with you. Why would you want someone that doesn't want you? If someone loves and treats you right and you love them, what more can you ask for? What more do you need? One man has given you his heart, which is the sun. Why must he give you the stars and the moon too, when the competition is offering nothing but heartache? There's nothing to wonder about at this point. The decision should be easy.

"When a man loves a woman, it's apparent. There is no gray area. If past trauma prevents someone from loving or treating you the way you deserved to be treated, you have no choice but to move on. You can trick yourself into believing that you have unbelievable chemistry with someone that can't be surpassed or duplicated, but that's a lie. Chemistry is cool and all, but it's no match for real love, which is loyalty and an everlasting commitment to grow together. Don't sacrifice the great relationship you have with Darren for a dream that exists when you are asleep but is never present when you are awake. Marriage is a lifelong commitment, and your spouse shouldn't be in second place or some consolation prize that you settle for because you got tired of waiting on the person you really want to be with. Just as you desire and require someone's whole heart, Darren has earned and deserves the same in return."

As Tee pondered my words, she clasped her hands together and nodded in agreement. After contemplating my words for a few additional moments, she eventually uttered, "Prince, why do you think Hassan and I never gave what could be a chance?"

"Tee, I must truly love you like a sister because I'm about to break the bro code for the first time ever. You and I both know that Hassan is an extremely complicated person. He's afraid to love because he fears experiencing the pain that sometimes comes with loss. Some people deal with loss by doing whatever they can to ensure that they never lose again. Being in love requires being vulnerable in a way that is susceptible to creating a potential loss that some people aren't willing to live with. You and I both know why Hassan is unwilling to risk another substantial loss. I know you and Hassan love each other dearly, but it's pretty apparent that your love for one another is destined to remain in the friendship apparatus and not evolve into the romantic realm. You have to ask yourself why you need your love for Hassan to be something more than it is. You have friendship love in Hassan and romantic love with Darren. What more do you want?"

"Indubitably," Tee replied as she seemingly analyzed my every word. "Prince, how did you know that your wife was the one?"

While chuckling at Tee's deflection, I reflected on my first date with my wife. "Tee, I knew she was the one when she said Santino was her favorite player in the NBA during our first date. She didn't even know that he was my boy. She had no idea that we grew up together, but for some reason, he was her favorite player." After I finished my statement about Santino being my wife's favorite player, Tee and I both burst out laughing. "Your wife knows her stuff. Tino is a bad boy. Tree Port's finest, a bad boy on that basketball court for sure."

After we regained our composure, she stated, "Prince, one last question. Before you got married, how did you know that your marriage was the right move? How did you know that your union was capable of standing the test of time?"

"You want me to be politically correct, or you want the truth?" I asked.

Without speaking, Tee nodded her head and mouthed, "The T-R-U-T-H."

"Tee, truth be told, going into my marriage, I didn't know that it was going to last. I was hopeful that it would, but I didn't know for sure until my marriage was upside down and I was unexpectedly on the brink of divorce. No one cheated. Neither one of us did anything crazy. We just started to grow apart in this organic way where being married and in the same household was no longer fun or enjoyable. We evolved into a functional marriage that was hyper-focused on taking care of our kids and finances. So much so that our marriage started to suffer from mutual benign neglect that made us both feel unappreciated. Tee, my marriage was on the verge of collapsing, so much so, I contacted the best divorce lawyer in the business. I had a divorce consultation with The Law Office of Ashanti A. Lilley. It took me contacting a divorce lawyer to finally realize that I was about to give up on my amazing wife and family without fully giving it my all. I couldn't do it."

Reminiscing on that candid conversation about friendship and marriage while sitting in the passenger seat of Tee's car gave me the courage I needed. I let Tee know that I needed her to be my getaway driver because I was going to kill Renlo. "Tee, to save Hassan from self-destructing, I have to do something about Renlo. He's fresh out of prison, and Hassan is determined to kill him. Hassan is too emotional to carry out the killing without leaving some sort of paper trail that leads back to our crew, which would cause a war and the loss of too many innocent lives." Tee was no fan of violence, and neither was I, but it was the only way in my estimation that we could end Hassan's quest for vengeance that was driving him crazier by the second.

"Prince, just give me the directions," she stated as she shifted from park to drive and headed north. I needed Tee to be my driver because the whole West End knew what type of car I drove, and Tee's tinted windows made her the perfect getaway driver. As Tee and I headed to our destination, so many thoughts raced through my mind. I was about to become what I had worked so hard to avoid becoming. I was about to become a brother who takes the life of another black man. Everything that I stood for was about to be erased because I cared for my best friend Hassan's wellbeing so much, and I partially blamed myself for his mental state. While what I was about to do felt wrong, I knew it was the right thing to do. I could shoulder the burden of being a murderer so long as I knew that my actions were the last resort and for the greater good. I would be killing a murderer that was fresh out of prison after all. As I contemplated the prospect of killing a man from the Tree Port community who shared my complexion, my mind drifted to a conversation that the Nothing to Lose Crew had on the block one day.

One evening as the daylight became entangled with the descending darkness of the night, the Nothing to Lose crew congregated on the block and shot the bull while the spring breeze soothed us. On that particular evening, I remember Hassan showing up to the block and asking the squad a random question about heaven and hell that threw us all for an unexpected loop. Apparently, earlier that day, Hassan and his dad had a conversation about America being hell for the black man. Hassan's conversation with his father rattled and troubled him so much that he sought us out and proceeded to ask a question that probably should have never been asked. Hassan's question should have remained a passing thought because the question he asked us led to one of those circular conspiracy conversations that occur in every black barbershop on Saturdays.

"Yo! Prince, Marcus, Rock and Tino, do any of y'all believe in heaven and hell?" an out of breath Hassan inquired as we gathered around him.

Dumbfounded by the question, Marcus was the first brave soul that attempted to answer the question. "Absolutely, not. There's no way heaven and hell are real. You mean to tell me the creator of the universe, an all-knowing God, spoke heaven into existence and then proceeded to create Adam and Eve so that he can send some of us to hell for a sin that Eve committed. You telling me I deserve to die and burn in hell because Adam's wife ate an apple that a snake implored her to eat? If a snake could talk then, why can't snakes talk now? I rest my case."

Santino quickly interjected. "Ignore the fool that is Marcus. He clearly smokes entirely too much. His brain cells are completely fried, and he's definitely going to hell when he dies."

"I mean, if hell is real, at least I would get to light my blunt up with hell's fire without ever asking to borrow a lighter," Marcus quipped back at Tino while suspending his hands in the air in a who cares manner that indicated that he didn't care where he was going when he died.

"I think y'all take some of the stories in the Bible too literal. The B.I.B.L.E. is simply our Basic Instructions Before Leaving Earth. You read it to learn lessons that should teach you how to be a better person so long as you glean the right messages from it. It doesn't matter if the snake was real or if the serpent could actually talk. The snake symbolizes that we are all susceptible to falling victim to temptation. When you read literature, you have to use common sense to understand it. Heaven and hell are real, from my perspective. Heaven is in your heart, and hell is here on earth. Humans are conflicted beings who have the potential to be good or evil at all times. It's up to each individual to decide if they want to follow the lead of their higher conscience (good) or succumb to their lower conscience (evil). I think we are all on a journey to become the best versions of ourselves, but we are often derailed from our path because we are willing to give in to carnal desires such as greed, selfishness, murder and a litany of other harmful acts that embody evil to advance in life. Every person standing here has free will; therefore, we must decide if we want to live up to our higher selves, which is the God in us or give in to our lower conscience, which is evil. Think about Lucifer. He was in heaven, a perfect place filled with joy and happiness, but his free will and selfish desires led to jealousy, which caused him to envy God. How could evil and jealously exist in Lucifer before Eve ever ate from the forbidden tree? That lets you know that even in heaven, the perfect place to be, that free will existed before humans were created and the potential for evil or giving in to one's lower conscience already existed."

As we all pondered Santino's interesting perspective, I decided to share my take on heaven and hell. "I honestly don't know if heaven and hell exist in the context that we are taught. Think about it. We have this relationship with God that doesn't operate or exist in the same way as it did with the Bible's characters. When the Bible was written, God spoke so clearly and talked so frequently that several different individuals were able to write full-fledged books of the gospel based on the information that God relayed to them. Why was it so easy for the authors of the Bible to hear from God back then, but in this day and age, no one can clearly articulate how we are supposed to hear from God? It's like back then, it was so easy to tell God was real, but now we have to rely on a book and preachers that claim they are called by God. I don't think we are taught the right way to communicate with God, so even if God does exist, our words may not reach him."

On that evening, everyone had so many questions about God, heaven, hell and the true meaning of life. For as much thinking as I did about life and making the world a better place, I don't think I ever understood the meaning of life until that fateful day when I failed to kill Renlo and ended up killing

Hassan.

When Tee drove me to where Renlo was on what would become the worst day of my life, I was determined to kill him no matter what. As I clutched my gun while reclining in the passenger seat of Tee's car, I patiently waited for her to give me the green light that Renlo was exiting the apartment complex where the mother of his child lived. As soon as his Air Force Ones hit the last step that led to the entrance of the complex, Tee nodded her head and whispered, "That's him."

As soon as Tee said, "that's him," I immediately jumped up from the reclining seat, cocked my gun to put a bullet in the chamber and moved my left hand to the silver car door lever to make my exit. Just as I was opening the car door, Tee grabbed my hand that was holding the gun and shrieked, "Prince, he has his son with him!"

While I was shocked by this turn of events, I wasn't going to let that deter me from my ultimate goal. I shook my head from side to side and said, "Tee, it doesn't matter. I have perfect aim. I won't harm his son. This is going to be a straight headshot that kills Renlo instantly. He won't even have time to ask God for the forgiveness of his sins. I'm going to make sure he burns in hell."

A frantic Tee gripped my left hand with all her might and refused to let me make a smooth exit from her car. As precious seconds were wasted, Tee continued to wrestle and plead with me until, eventually, my target entered his vehicle and was able to drive off without encountering the Angel of Death that I had morphed into. Once Renlo made his getaway, Tee and I just sat there in disbelief. No words were exchanged. She just drove me back to my office, the place where Hassan was waiting for me to deliver the news that would change his life for the better.

Instead of entering my office with good news, I had to share the information that shattered my best friend's world. The terrible news that I shared pushed Hassan over the edge. I had broken my promise. I had failed to kill Renlo. Before I got the chance to explain the situation, sheer anger and disappointment took a complete hold on Hassan's psyche. While ignoring every word and explanation that I offered and the promise that I would keep my word to kill Renlo, Hassan pulled out his pistol and aimed it directly at my head. That's how it all happened. That was how my best friend ended up in heaven and associated with my case. I killed Hassan because I felt I had to. Now we were both in heaven before the judge of all judges who had declared that one of us had to go hell. Either it was self-defense, which meant that the murdered person forced the other person's hand and would have to spend eternity in hell. Or it was murder, which meant I would spend eternity in hell for violating the most important commandment, "Thou Shall Not Kill."

12

PEACE KING

When my trek with the ageless Being concluded, we arrived in front of what appeared to be heaven's courtroom. The Eternal Being extended his hands and commanded the gold and heavenly scarlet doors to open without uttering a word or touching them. As I entered the courtroom, I saw an older and withered version of the individual that discharged the treacherous bullet that erased my name from the book of life during my late twenties. I saw my ace from the sandbox, my long-lost friend Prince. As odd as it may sound, I felt no hate or animosity towards him. I understood why he did what he did. He ended my life to prevent a war that would have cost our hood and the West End countless lives. Prince's actions were consistently for the greater good of Tree Port. He longed for an environment where there were no gunshots, a place where children could play and enjoy life freely without worrying about a bullet with no real direction ending their life prematurely. A space that permitted grandmas and granddads to happily walk the sidewalks of Tree Port at night without the fear of being robbed hovering all around them.

While entering the courtroom, it finally dawned on me. Prince had requested me as his lawyer in heaven on his day of judgment. I had spent what I thought was just a few hours or so asking the ageless Being a multitude of questions about life as we headed towards what I now realized was heaven's courtroom. Apparently, time elapsed differently on earth versus heaven. A few hours in heaven translated to a few decades on earth.

As I approached Prince, he stood up confidently, cracked a happy as can be smile and extended his right hand for a handshake and stated, "One more case. One final legal entanglement for the only lawyer capable of defeating God." Prince had seen me secure the freedom of eleven individuals as he had attended all the verdict days for the cases that I took on. While his confidence in my ability to free him was refreshing, I was petrified. Gone was the tremendous confidence that I had acquired from my previous courtroom victories on earth. Instead, fear and doubt gripped my heart as we waited to hear from the Creator.

"Prince, how did you end up here? How did you pass away?" I inquired.

"Old age, I suppose. I went to sleep last night and woke

up here instead of in bed beside my beautiful wife." Before continuing, it seemed Prince's thoughts drifted to fond memories of his wife Michelle as he stared beyond me as if I was made of glass. Eventually, his focus shifted from the past back to the present, and he continued speaking. "I made it to my sixties, which is probably at least eighty in all other communities outside of Tree Port. That has to count for something, right?" he stated as he chuckled.

I laughed out loud while uttering, "true."

"How long have you been here?" Prince asked.

"I'm not sure. Not too long, I guess. It feels like it's the same day that I departed Earth. Did you have an opportunity to chop it up with the Eternal Being who seems to have an answer for every question in the universe?"

Prince replied, "Yep," while nodding his head. "I was able to get a few questions in while we were walking or gliding this way.

"I asked him if God was married, and the Being told me, 'Does God seem dumb enough to get married only to risk losing half of heaven in a divorce? Nobody is staying happily married for eternity, not even God.' "

As I pondered the information that Prince shared regarding God and marriage, I asked him what other questions he asked the Being.

Prince continued, "I asked him if Black people would

ever obtain true freedom and equality in America.

"What was the Being's response?" I inquired.

Prince replied, "He kept it real. The Eternal Being told me:

'Your people cannot and will not obtain freedom so long as they continue to cling to the idea that the American Dream is real and not a nightmare. Just like there were people in Israel who chose to remain in bondage instead of following Moses, some African Americans will not choose freedom. They will fight and oppose the march towards freedom because they believe in the idea of America more than they love themselves. It's one of the everlasting effects of slavery. They say to themselves, how can I provide for myself if I lose my job? They don't honestly believe that God is Jehovah Jireh, their provider. Has God failed to give you the understanding and knowledge of how to plant a seed? If you know how to plant a seed, you shall always be able to harvest. Has he that is greater in you failed to give you the understanding and wisdom of how to fish? If a man knows how to fish, how can he starve? I say to you. You are choosing hell over heaven because you know not of the greatness of heaven because you have only seen and lived in the hell that is America. America keeps trying to destroy herself, but you (black people) keep intervening to save her. If you want true freedom, you must let America destroy itself. You claim to want radical change and a revolution, yet you maintain the status quo in how you think and vote.' "

After Prince and I finished sharing the conversations we had with the Eternal Being with one another, we sat quietly in our seats until a thunderous voice or internal thought we assumed was the Alpha and Omega began to speak. The voice with no face detailed the murder charge that Prince was accused of and informed him that today was his day of judgement. This was the day that would determine our eternal place of residence.

"On the Ides of March, Prince Lamar Smith, you desecrated the ultimate commandment, *Thou Shall Not Kill*. My commandment and words are clear. Under no circumstances should a man take the life of another man, woman, or child. Do you acknowledge that you have committed murder and accept eternal damnation to hell as your punishment, or would you like an opportunity to present a defense that explains why you decided to play God?"

Hearing God's voice is hard to describe. It's eerily similar to the internal intuition we occasionally hear in our minds that tends to pop up in dire circumstances to steer us in the right direction.

Hearing God's voice appeared to startle Prince as he didn't reply promptly. As Prince remained silent, I stood up and stated, "Prince is not guilty of murder. He's no different than Abraham. Abraham was willing to sacrifice his own son's life to obey you. Prince was following his God-given ethics to prevent a street war that would have resulted in scores of lives being lost. Is one life lost in good faith not worth it if it prevents the loss of countless lives? Prince sacrificed my life to defend the lives of others in Tree Port. In essence, it was self-defense. I would argue that it was the good in him, the voice of God that told him to sacrifice my life as you commanded Abraham to sacrifice Issac." After I completed my comparison of Prince's actions versus Abraham's actions, God nonchalantly dismissed my first argument and offered no exoneration for Prince's act. Disappointed that my compelling defense had failed to resonate with God, I stood up and presented another view.

"How can a fair and just God in good conscience send a black man to hell for eternity when this black man has already spent his entire life in hell? Sending an African American man who has already spent 60 years residing in America to hell for eternity is Double Jeopardy. Prince just survived hell, so why would you send him back to hell? He was subjected to systemic oppression, racism, police violence and countless other injustices in America. He should be rewarded with immunity in the afterlife for surviving as a black man in America. His act of violence is the direct result of oppression in America and God's failure to act on our behalf for four hundred plus years. Should he have let me live and let others die?

"During this constant war that America has waged against black people, God has mostly remained silent. Anytime we wake up in the morning to see another day, we thank you. When cops murder our unarmed family members or friends, we forgive as you have commanded us to do. Anytime we experience a win, we give you the glory. It must be nice to get all the credit for all the good in the world but never receive any blame for the bad that happens. Was it not an oversight by God that allowed Lucifer to exist in heaven in the first place? Before Eve ever ate the forbidden fruit, sin already existed by virtue of the jealousy that lived in Lucifer when he was in heaven. Do you not hold yourself accountable for allowing the father of all lies to reside in heaven in the first place? Just as you decided to take action against the devil and the third of angels that chose to follow him, Prince decided to take action and stand up for what's right by removing me from the equation.

"Once again, I'm asking how a just God can sit idly by while innocent black people are subjected to slavery, rape, murder, Jim Crow and several other acts of violence and expect the oppressed to never respond to such actions. Prince's decision to kill me is inextricably connected to the systemic oppression that creates neighborhoods where violence is high. We didn't choose these communities for ourselves or develop them under our own volition. If school districts were equally funded, Prince would have never ended up in a predicament where he had to consider ending my life to save the lives of others. Prince had a difficult decision to make, but he made the right decision. Take a life and save innocent lives in Tree Port, or let a destructive war take place. He did the same thing you did when you cast Lucifer out of heaven for the greater good.

"Secondly, how is Prince's act any different than your decision to sacrifice your son's life to save the lives of others? Can you not relate to a man who loves his community so much that he is willing to sacrifice anything to save it?

"How can God, in good conscience, sit and listen to his children in America, pray, cry out and beg for assistance for four hundred plus years and refuse to act on their behalf? Black people on earth are starting to question if you exist. If we are unsure of your existence due to your silence and inaction, how could Prince even know that the 'Thou Shall Not Kill' commandment was real and the importance of following it?

"In closing, I need you to understand that it is unfair and wrong to send a black man to hell for eternity when he has already resided in the hell that is America."

A few moments after my closing argument, the judge

and jury of life and death reached a verdict. "Mr. Johnson, while your argument was profound, there will be no exceptions. One of you must be found guilty and sentenced to hell. When a murder is committed, it either has to be justified as self-defense for the perpetrator to enter the pearly gates, or the perpetrator of the act must be found guilty of committing murder and ultimately sentenced to eternal damnation."

My heart sunk as I realized that there was no way for both Prince and me to enter heaven. I took a deep breath as tears started to flow from my face and spoke directly to Prince. "Prince, tell my little brother Deuce how much I love him. Tell him how sorry I am that I couldn't protect him. Tell him how much I love him. Greater love hath no man than this, that a man lay down his life for his friends."

As I found the courage to speak while tears of pain continued to fall, I accepted hell as my eternal fate and spoke to God. "Prince was justified in taking my life. It was self-defense."

ABOUT THE AUTHOR

Marquise Thompson was born and raised in Gastonia, North Carolina. Marquise is a thoughtful dreamer that takes pride in using his words and creative view of life to inspire others to think outside of the box. Being a father, husband, and advocate for black people's growth and development are his most immense joys in life. He strongly believes that the journey to greatness begins within and that we must all become the best versions of ourselves to make the world a better place.